Frozen Future: Elemental Truths of Arctic Global Warming

Steele Andrew Darren

Published by Steele Andrew Darren, 2024.

While every precaution has been taken in the preparation of this book, the publisher assumes no responsibility for errors or omissions, or for damages resulting from the use of the information contained herein.

FROZEN FUTURE: ELEMENTAL TRUTHS OF ARCTIC GLOBAL WARMING

First edition. March 15, 2024.

Copyright © 2024 Steele Andrew Darren.

ISBN: 979-8224969913

Written by Steele Andrew Darren.

Table of Contents

Chapter 1: Introduction- Brief Overview of Global Warming

1.1 Background

Global warming has been a topic of great concern for scientists, policymakers, and the general public in recent decades. The term refers to the long-term increase in Earth's average surface temperature, primarily caused by human activities. These activities predominantly involve the burning of fossil fuels such as coal, oil, and natural gas, which release greenhouse gases (GHGs) into the atmosphere. The major GHG implicated in global warming is carbon dioxide (CO_2).

1.2 Historical Context

The notion of global warming began to garner scientific attention in the late 19th century, with the work of Swedish scientist Svante Arrhenius. He discovered the warming effect of CO_2 and predicted that doubling its concentration in the atmosphere would lead to a significant increase in global temperatures. However, it wasn't until the latter half of the 20th century that widespread concern about global warming started to emerge.

1.3 The Greenhouse Effect

Before delving deeper into the explanation of global warming, it is essential to understand the concept of the greenhouse effect. The Earth's atmosphere acts as a blanket, trapping certain wavelengths of heat radiation and keeping the planet warm. This is possible due to the presence of GHGs like CO_2, methane (CH_4), nitrous oxide (N_2O), and chlorofluorocarbons (CFCs), which absorb and re-emit this heat, preventing it from escaping into space.

1.4 Anthropogenic Influence

While natural factors such as volcanic activity and solar radiation have contributed to past climate variations, the current rapid warming trend can be attributed primarily to human activities. Industrialization and the associated increase in the burning of fossil fuels have released substantial amounts of CO_2, intensifying the greenhouse effect and leading to an overabundance of GHGs in the atmosphere.

1.5 Widespread Impacts

The consequences of global warming can already be observed across the planet. Rising sea levels, more frequent and intense heatwaves, droughts, floods, and extreme weather events are just a few examples. The warming process also affects ecosystems and biodiversity, disrupts agriculture, and poses serious risks to human health. These impacts are projected to worsen in the coming decades if greenhouse gas emissions remain uncontrolled.

1.6 International Efforts

Recognizing the seriousness of global warming and its potential for catastrophic consequences, global leaders have sought to address the issue. The international community has come together under various frameworks, such as the United Nations Framework Convention on Climate Change (UNFCCC) and its subsequent agreement, the Paris Agreement. These initiatives aim to mitigate GHG emissions and promote adaptation strategies to cope with the existing and anticipated impacts of global warming.

1.7 Chapter Overview

This chapter provides a brief overview of global warming, highlighting its background, causes, impacts, and the international efforts to combat it. The subsequent chapters in this book will delve deeper into these topics, exploring the scientific evidence, technological solutions, and policy measures needed to address this global challenge effectively.

In conclusion, this introductory chapter sets the stage by presenting a comprehensive overview of global warming. It establishes the significance of the issue, outlines its causes and impacts, and highlights the global response to mitigate and adapt to this pressing concern. Armed with this foundation, the subsequent chapters will delve further into the complexity of the subject matter, providing a deeper understanding of the scientific, social, and economic aspects surrounding global warming.

- Importance of studying global warming in the Arctic

As we examine the phenomenon of global warming, it becomes evident that one of the crucial regions to focus on is the Arctic. The extreme cold environment, unique ecosystems, and potential catastrophic consequences make studying global warming in the Arctic of utmost importance. By understanding the impacts on this sensitive region, scientists can gain valuable insights that aid in predicting and mitigating the effects on global climate.

The Arctic region, often referred to as the "canary in the coal mine" for global climate change, experiences more dynamic shifts in temperature than any other area on Earth. Over the past few decades, it has witnessed a substantially larger increase in average temperatures compared to the global average. This rapid warming has severe repercussions for the fragile ecosystems and indigenous communities that call this region home.

One of the most significant concerns of global warming in the Arctic is melting sea ice. The Arctic sea ice serves as a highly reflective surface that reflects incoming solar radiation back into space. However, due to rising temperatures, sea ice is melting at an alarming rate. As ice cover decreases, a larger portion of the sun's energy is absorbed by the darker ocean, leading to further warming and ice melt. This positive feedback loop intensifies the warming in the region and can have extensive impacts on global climate patterns.

The melting of sea ice also has direct consequences for wildlife and ecosystems in the Arctic. Species such as polar bears depend on sea ice for hunting and reproduction, and with diminishing ice cover, their survival is threatened. Furthermore, the loss of ice negatively impacts marine mammals like seals and walruses, disrupting the delicate balance of the Arctic food web. Studying these dynamic ecosystem changes is vital as it allows us to comprehend the complexity of interconnections and predict the cascading effects on other species in the region and beyond.

Another critical aspect to consider when studying global warming in the Arctic is its potential feedback on the global climate system. The Arctic holds vast amounts of carbon in permafrost and undersea sediments, accumulated over thousands of years. As temperatures rise, this organic material thaws, releasing greenhouse gases, primarily carbon dioxide and methane, into the atmosphere. These potent greenhouse gases further contribute to global warming, amplifying climate change not only in the Arctic but also on a global scale. Understanding these feedback mechanisms is crucial to accurately modeling and mitigating the effects of global warming around the world.

While the importance of studying global warming in the Arctic is apparent, it is essential to recognize the challenges associated with this research. Conducting studies in this harsh and remote environment presents logistical difficulties and significant financial investments. Access to data and adequate research platforms are limited due to the remote location and the extreme weather conditions.

Nonetheless, advancements in technology and international cooperation have paved the way for sustained monitoring and exploration of the Arctic region. Satellites, automated buoys, and research vessels together provide valuable information that helps scientists make informed predictions for the future.

In conclusion, understanding the impacts of global warming in the Arctic is paramount to comprehend the consequences for the global climate system. Through studying the unique ecosystems, tracking sea ice melt, and investigating carbon feedbacks, scientists can gain critical insights into the mechanisms and potential consequences of climate change. This knowledge is crucial for developing effective mitigation strategies and policies to combat global warming and preserve the delicate balance of our planet.

Chapter 2: Understanding Global Warming

Global warming, the increase in the average temperature of the Earth's atmosphere, has been a topic of great importance and concern in recent years. It is a complex phenomenon influenced by various factors and has significant implications for the future of our planet. In this chapter, we will delve into the intricacies of global warming, examining its causes, effects, and potential solutions.

To understand global warming, it is critical to comprehend the greenhouse effect. The greenhouse effect refers to the trapping of heat by certain gases within the Earth's atmosphere, such as carbon dioxide (CO_2) and methane (CH_4). These gases act as a blanket, preventing the escape of heat into space and thereby leading to an overall rise in temperature. While this natural phenomenon is essential for sustaining life on Earth, human activities have intensified it, resulting in an enhanced greenhouse effect and subsequently, global warming.

Several human activities contribute to the increase in greenhouse gases and, consequently, global warming. The burning of fossil fuels for energy production, industrial processes, and transportation is a major contributor. When fossil fuels such as coal, oil, and natural gas are burnt, they release large amounts of CO_2 into the atmosphere. Deforestation is another significant factor as trees serve as carbon sinks, absorbing CO_2 from the atmosphere. Furthermore, agricultural practices, particularly livestock farming and the use of synthetic fertilizers, result in the release of methane, a potent greenhouse gas.

The consequences of global warming are far-reaching and pose serious challenges to both the environment and human society. One of the most immediate effects is the rise in global temperatures. The past few decades have witnessed record-breaking heat waves, warmest years on record, and melting of glaciers and polar ice caps. Rising temperatures have led to shifts in precipitation patterns, resulting in more frequent and intense droughts, floods, and storms, which threaten agriculture, water resources, and human settlements.

Moreover, global warming impacts ecosystems and biodiversity. The rising temperatures and changing climate conditions disrupt natural habitats, forcing some species to migrate or face extinction. Coral reefs, which support an astonishing array of marine life, are extremely vulnerable to increased ocean temperatures and acidification, with many already experiencing severe bleaching events.

The alarming effects of global warming have prompted actions and policy interventions to mitigate its extent and impact. International agreements, such as the Paris Agreement, aim to limit global temperature rise to well below 2 degrees Celsius above pre-industrial levels. This necessitates a transition to cleaner and renewable sources of energy, such as solar and wind power, as well as energy efficiency measures. Additionally, efforts to conserve forests, implement sustainable agricultural practices, and promote the use of cleaner technologies are crucial steps towards curbing global warming.

In conclusion, understanding global warming involves a comprehensive analysis of its causes, effects, and potential solutions. Human activities, particularly the burning of fossil fuels and deforestation, have exacerbated the greenhouse effect, leading to a rise in global temperatures. The consequences of global warming include extreme weather events, dwindling natural resources, and threats to ecosystems and biodiversity. However, concerted efforts to reduce greenhouse gas emissions, embrace renewable energy, and adopt sustainable practices offer hope for a sustainable future. It is our duty as global citizens to acknowledge the importance of fighting global warming and to take timely action to protect our planet for future generations.

- Definition and causes of global warming

Definition:
Global warming refers to the gradual increase in the Earth's average temperature due to human activities, specifically the emission of greenhouse gases into the atmosphere. This phenomenon has been observed across the globe and has significant implications for the planet's ecosystems and climate patterns.

Causes:

1. Greenhouse gases: Various gases, such as carbon dioxide (CO_2), methane (CH_4), nitrous oxide (N_2O), and ozone (O_3), form a layer in the Earth's atmosphere known as the greenhouse effect. While this natural process is necessary for regulating the planet's temperature, human activities have increased the concentration of these gases, intensifying the greenhouse effect and leading to global warming. The primary activities contributing to the rise in greenhouse gases include burning fossil fuels (coal, oil, and natural gas) for electricity and transportation, deforestation, and excessive industrialization.

2. Deforestation: The clearing of forests significantly contributes to global warming. Forests play a vital role in absorbing carbon dioxide from the atmosphere. However, widespread deforestation eliminates these natural sinks, resulting in an accumulation of CO_2 and reducing the planet's ability to regulate its temperature.

3. Industrialization: The rapid industrial growth witnessed in recent decades has led to increased emissions of greenhouse gases. Heavy machinery, manufacturing processes, and power generators emit large quantities of CO_2 and other pollutants. The use of non-renewable energy sources, such as coal-fired power plants or oil-based industries, further accelerates global warming.

4. Agricultural practices: Activities related to modern agriculture, such as the use of synthetic fertilizers, livestock farming, and waste management, release substantial amounts of methane and nitrous oxide. Methane is emitted through natural processes in livestock and in the storage and transport of

manure, while nitrous oxide is released from the breakdown of nitrogen-based fertilizers. These gases are potent contributors to the greenhouse effect, intensifying global warming.

5. Rapid population growth: With the exponential growth of the global population, there has been an increase in energy consumption and resource utilization. This population growth translates into higher demands for transportation, electricity, and consumer goods, all of which require the burning of fossil fuels, thereby aggravating global warming.

6. Urbanization: Rapid urbanization leads to the concentrated release of greenhouse gases due to increased energy consumption by residential buildings, transportation systems, industries, and waste management. The urban heat island effect, where cities experience significantly higher temperatures than the surrounding rural areas, further amplifies global warming.

7. Industrial and agricultural waste disposal: Improper management and disposal of industrial and agricultural waste contribute to global warming. Dumping waste in landfills results in the emission of methane as organic waste decomposes. Additionally, ineffective waste management practices in livestock farming allow methane emissions from manure storages and waste disposal systems.

It is important to note that global warming is a complex issue with multiple interconnected causes. The urgency to address global warming lies in its far-reaching consequences, including rising sea levels, extreme weather events, biodiversity loss, and disruption to ecosystems. Mitigating global warming requires concerted efforts to reduce greenhouse gas emissions through renewable energy sources, sustainable agriculture, afforestation, and implementing policies that promote environmentally friendly practices.

- Exploration of greenhouse gases

Exploration of greenhouse gases is a topic that has gained significant attention in recent years due to their detrimental effects on the environment and climate. Greenhouse gases refer to a group of gases that are responsible for trapping heat within the Earth's atmosphere, leading to the greenhouse effect. This effect is a natural process and is vital for sustaining life on our planet. However, the increased concentration of these gases in the atmosphere, primarily due to human activities, has resulted in an intensification of the greenhouse effect, leading to global warming and climate change.

The main greenhouse gases of concern include carbon dioxide (CO_2), methane (CH_4), nitrous oxide (N_2O), and fluorinated gases. Carbon dioxide is the most prominent greenhouse gas and is primarily generated through the burning of fossil fuels such as coal, oil, and natural gas. Other significant contributors include deforestation and industrial processes. Methane, on the other hand, has a short lifespan but is more potent in trapping heat, making it responsible for almost 16% of the global warming potential. It is predominantly produced in agricultural activities, waste management processes, and the extraction and use of fossil fuels. Nitrous oxide is mainly emitted through agricultural and industrial activities, whereas fluorinated gases are human-made gases produced through industrial processes and are used as substitutes for ozone-depleting substances.

Understanding the composition, sources, and effects of greenhouse gases has become essential for developing effective strategies to mitigate their concentration in the atmosphere. This has led to extensive research and exploration conducted to collect data and assess the impact of greenhouse gases on the environment.

Scientists and researchers have deployed various measurement techniques and instruments to quantify the concentration of greenhouse gases in the atmosphere. These measurement techniques include ground-based monitoring stations, satellites, aircraft, and mobile laboratories. Ground-based monitoring stations provide real-time data on the atmospheric concentrations of greenhouse gases and are often strategically positioned to capture variations across different regions and ecosystems. Satellites equipped with specialized sensors have also greatly contributed to greenhouse gas monitoring by providing a global perspective and monitoring large-scale changes in the composition of the atmosphere over extended periods.

During exploration efforts, scientists collect data on the emission sources, distribution, atmospheric lifetime, and sinks (removal mechanisms) of greenhouse gases. This information is crucial to enhance climate models and accurately forecast future climate scenarios. Exploration activities span diverse regions, including forests, peatlands, wetlands, cities, and coastal areas, in order to understand the complex interactions between greenhouse gases and the natural as well as human-driven systems.

Furthermore, exploration of greenhouse gases goes beyond monitoring and measuring concentrations. Scientists also aim to explore innovative ways to reduce emissions and develop sustainable alternatives. These initiatives involve research into renewable energy sources, optimizing energy efficiency in various sectors, implementing carbon capture and storage technologies, and promoting sustainable land use practices, among others.

In conclusion, the exploration of greenhouse gases is a critical field of study that seeks to understand the composition, sources, and effects of these gases on the environment. Through extensive research and monitoring efforts, scientists aim to create strategies to mitigate their concentration in the atmosphere and prevent further damage to our planet's climate system. Exploration in this area not only provides valuable data for policymakers and scientists but also allows for the development of innovative solutions to combat the challenge of global warming and climate change.

- Impact of global warming on the environment

Global warming refers to the gradual increase in the Earth's temperature primarily caused by the release of greenhouse gases such as carbon dioxide (CO2) into the atmosphere. This phenomenon is primarily the result of human activities, such as burning fossil fuels and deforestation. The impact of global warming on the environment is far-reaching and has the potential to disrupt numerous ecosystems on Earth.

One of the most visible consequences of global warming is the rapidly melting glaciers and polar ice caps. This process directly contributes to rising sea levels worldwide. As sea levels rise, coastal areas, including densely populated cities, are at a higher risk of experiencing flooding, erosion, and saltwater intrusion. Small islands and low-lying regions are especially vulnerable and may face the threat of complete submersion.

Global warming also produces changes in weather patterns and extreme weather events. The higher levels of energy and moisture in the atmosphere lead to increased frequency and intensity of storms, hurricanes, and cyclones. This can cause devastation to human settlements, destroy infrastructure, and result in the loss of lives. Furthermore, changing weather patterns disrupt agricultural practices, leading to reductions in crop yields and food shortages in some regions.

Another significant consequence of global warming is the destruction of natural habitats and loss of biodiversity. Many species depend on specific temperature ranges and environmental conditions to survive, and as those conditions change rapidly due to global warming, many species face great challenges in adapting or finding new habitats. This has resulted in the extinction or endangerment of various plant and animal species. The loss of biodiversity disrupts entire ecosystems, affecting pollination, nutrient cycling, and other essential ecological processes.

Furthermore, the rise in global temperatures has contributed to the acidification of the oceans. Increased CO2 levels in the atmosphere can dissolve in seawater, forming carbonic acid. This acidification affects marine life, particularly coral reefs and shell-forming organisms like oysters, clams, and mussels. These organisms struggle to form their calcium carbonate shells or skeletons, threatening their survival and the delicate balance of marine ecosystems they inhabit.

Global warming also affects human health in several ways. Higher temperatures can lead to heatwaves, causing heat strokes and other heat-related illnesses. Additionally, the proliferation of disease-carrying insects, such as mosquitoes, is facilitated by warmer temperatures and altered climatic conditions. This raises the risk of diseases like malaria, dengue fever, and West Nile virus spreading to new regions.

To mitigate the impact of global warming on the environment, various measures can be taken. The primary approach is to reduce greenhouse gas emissions, primarily CO2, through adopting renewable energy sources, improving energy efficiency, afforestation, and reforestation efforts. Additionally, adapting to the unavoidable consequences of global warming by implementing better water management systems, constructing flood barriers, and developing heat-resistant crop varieties are essential strategies.

In conclusion, global warming has profound effects on the environment. Rising temperatures contribute to melting glaciers, changing weather patterns, loss of biodiversity, ocean acidification, and pose risks to human health. It is crucial that immediate action is taken to mitigate greenhouse gas emissions and adapt to a changing climate. Protecting our planet's ecosystems is essential for the well-being of both current and future generations.

- Introduction to the Arctic as a vulnerable region

The Arctic encompasses a vast area of land and ocean, extending across the northernmost regions of North America, Europe, and Asia. Known for its extreme climate, unique wildlife, and breathtaking landscapes, the Arctic has always captivated those who explore or study this remote region. However, beyond its natural wonders, the Arctic holds a hidden vulnerability that is increasingly capturing the attention of scientists, policymakers, and the global community.

In recent decades, the Arctic has undergone significant changes, primarily driven by climate change. Largely considered the "canary in the coal mine" for global climate trends, the Arctic experiences some of the most pronounced impacts of rising temperatures. The region has witnessed a rapid decline in sea ice extent, with perennial ice dwindling at an alarming rate. The melting of sea ice not only disrupts the Arctic's delicate ecosystem but also exacerbates the pace of climate change worldwide.

The Arctic is home to numerous indigenous communities, whose cultural heritage and way of life have evolved symbiotically with the harsh environment over millennia. These communities face tremendous challenges in adapting to the changing Arctic, as melting ice and altered marine ecosystems affect their traditional hunting and fishing practices. Moreover, the melting permafrost poses a threat to their homes and infrastructure, destabilizing the very ground on which they depend.

While climate change poses significant challenges to Arctic communities, it also brings opportunities that are attracting global attention. The shrinking of ice offers new opportunities for resource extraction, including oil, gas, and minerals. As a consequence, the Arctic has become a potential battleground for economic and geopolitical interests. The region's strategic significance is rising as new shipping routes open up, allowing for shorter journeys between Asia and Europe.

Addressing the vulnerabilities of the Arctic requires international cooperation and a focus on sustainability. The resilience of the region's ecosystems and communities must be preserved as we transition to a low-carbon future. Furthermore, responsible governance of the Arctic's resources becomes paramount to prevent environmentally damaging operations and protect the rights and well-being of indigenous peoples.

Understanding the vulnerabilities of the Arctic is not only important for safeguarding this unique and essential region but also for grasping the broader implications of climate change. As the Arctic continues to change, its physical and social systems serve as a crucial touchstone to comprehend the interconnectedness of our planet and the urgency at hand.

In this introduction to the Arctic as a vulnerable region, we will delve deep into the ecological, societal, and geopolitical dynamics shaping this delicate corner of the globe. We will explore the impacts of climate change on the Arctic ecosystem, the challenges faced by indigenous communities, and the opportunities and risks associated with an evolving Arctic. By examining these facets, we hope to foster a comprehensive understanding of the Arctic's vulnerability and the imperative to protect and sustain its future.

Chapter 3: The Arctic's Unique Climate Conditions

Climate conditions in the Arctic are unlike any other region in the world, characterized by long, frigid winters and brief, cool summers. The extreme cold and vast expanses of ice create a unique ecosystem that is both stunning and fragile. In this chapter, we delve into the various factors that contribute to the Arctic's distinctive climate, exploring the dynamics behind its frozen landscapes and exploring the implications of climate change on this delicate environment.

One of the fundamental reasons behind the Arctic's chilling temperatures is its high latitude. Located near the North Pole, the Arctic receives much less solar energy compared to other parts of the globe. This results in lower overall temperatures, with average winter temperatures plummeting well below freezing, often reaching as low as -40 degrees Celsius (-40 degrees Fahrenheit). In summer, temperatures rise, but remain relatively cool compared to temperate or tropical climates.

The Arctic's unique topography, characterized by vast expanses of ice and snow, further contributes to its chilly conditions. Thick ice covers a significant portion of the Arctic Ocean and surrounding land areas throughout the year. The ice acts as a reflective surface, known as the "albedo effect," which means that it reflects a significant amount of sunlight back into space, preventing it from being absorbed by the Earth's surface. As a result, the Arctic remains colder than it would have been without the presence of ice, creating a self-sustaining cycle that perpetuates its icy climate.

Furthermore, the Arctic experiences what is known as polar night and polar day. During the winter months, the Arctic is plunged into prolonged darkness as the sun remains below the horizon for weeks or even months at a time. Conversely, in summer months, the region experiences continuous daylight, with the sun never fully setting. These extreme variations in daylight hours have profound effects on the Arctic's climate, impacting everything from sea ice formation and melt to the growth and reproduction of plants and animals.

The Arctic's unique climate conditions support a range of specialized flora and fauna that have adapted to its harsh environment. Hardy plant species like mosses, lichens, and low-lying shrubs dominate the landscape, specially adapted to survive in the frozen ground and acidic soils. Animal species have also undergone remarkable adaptations to the Arctic's hostile conditions. From the iconic polar bear to Antarctic woolly caterpillars, these creatures possess adaptations such as insulating fur, blubber, and thick layers of fat to withstand the cold, conserve heat, and facilitate swimming through icy waters.

However, the Arctic climate is not immune to change. Over the past century, human-induced climate change has caused significant shifts in the Arctic, with profound implications for both the inhabitants of the region and the global climate system. Increasing greenhouse gas emissions from human activities have caused the Arctic to warm at a rate two to three times faster than the global average, leading to the accelerated melting of sea ice. This not only directly impacts species that rely on ice for survival, such as seals and walruses but also has far-reaching consequences for the entire Arctic food web.

Alongside the ice's decline, changes in precipitation patterns, circulation patterns, and air temperature have also been observed, further altering the Arctic's climate dynamics. These changes are intricately linked to shifts in weather patterns beyond the Arctic Circle, affecting weather systems across the globe. Thus, the Arctic's unique climate conditions play a crucial role in the Earth's climate system, acting as a refrigerator that helps regulate global temperature and ocean currents.

In conclusion, the Arctic's climate conditions are fascinating and unparalleled. From its high latitude and extensive ice cover to the polar night and day cycles, the Arctic possesses a truly unique climate. However, the region now faces the imminent threat of climate change, which is fundamentally reshaping its fragile environment. Understanding and addressing the challenges posed by Arctic climate change is not only essential for the preservation of this remarkable ecosystem but also for the global climate system as a whole.

- Details on the unique climate characteristics of the Arctic

The Arctic region is renowned for its unique climate characteristics, which are truly unlike any other place on Earth. Here, the extremity of temperatures, geographic location, and the presence of polar ice create a distinct and captivating climate system.

One of the most defining features of the Arctic climate is its extreme cold temperatures. This frozen landscape experiences bitterly cold winters, with temperatures regularly plummeting below -30 degrees Celsius (-22 degrees Fahrenheit). In fact, the coldest temperature ever recorded was -68 degrees Celsius (-90 degrees Fahrenheit) in the Siberian village of Oymyakon in 1933. Such frigid conditions make this region one of the most hostile environments on the planet.

The Arctic is also characterized by its long, harsh winters and relatively short summers. The winter season here can last up to nine months, with darkness dominating the landscape for weeks on end. During this season, the sun hovers below the horizon for extended periods, creating an ethereal phenomenon known as the polar night. In contrast, the summer season brings the midnight sun, a majestic phenomenon where the sun remains visible 24 hours a day, providing almost continuous daylight. These drastic differences in sunlight exposure dramatically affect the local flora, fauna, and human inhabitants, shaping their livelihoods and survival strategies.

Furthermore, the presence of vast amounts of sea ice is a key component of the Arctic climate. The Arctic Ocean is covered with ice for the majority of the year, reaching its maximum extent during late winter and beginning to recede during summer. This ice cover plays a crucial role in regulating the Earth's climate system, reflecting incoming sunlight and helping to cool the atmosphere. However, the significant loss of Arctic sea ice due to climate change has disrupted this delicate balance, leading to rising sea levels, altered ocean currents, and changes in weather patterns around the world.

Interestingly, despite the extreme conditions, the Arctic region still experiences periods of warm temperatures during the summer months. The annual average temperature hovers around 0 degrees Celsius (32 degrees Fahrenheit) near the coasts but drops significantly further inland, where colder continental air masses prevail. These temporary warm periods provide an opportunity for plant life and animals to thrive, making the region a fantastic ecosystem for certain species. These unique adaptations have allowed various creatures like polar bears, Arctic foxes, and reindeer to survive and flourish in this harsh environoment.

The Arctic climate also plays a vital role in global weather patterns and climate change. Unexpected alterations in the Earth's climate, such as prolonged heatwaves or extreme weather events, are frequently attributed to changes occurring in the Arctic region. Given its sensitive nature and the accelerating impacts of climate change, studying its climate system has become increasingly crucial, not only for scientists but for humanity as a whole.

In conclusion, the Arctic climate encompasses various unique characteristics that define its exceptional nature. The extreme cold temperatures, long winters and short summers, expansive sea ice, and annual cycle of darkness and daylight are all elements that contribute to the distinctiveness of this region. As we witness the consequences of climate change unfolding in the Arctic, it becomes imperative to recognize the significance of its climate system and its role in shaping our planet's future.

- Examination of the Arctic's role in regulating global climate

The Arctic plays a vital role in regulating the Earth's climate system. Its unique characteristics and processes have a profound impact on global temperature patterns, oceanic circulation, and even weather systems in distant regions. This examination will explore some of the key factors that make the Arctic a crucial component of our planet's climate system.

One of the most significant ways in which the Arctic regulates global climate is through its extensive ice and snow cover. The polar ice caps, particularly the vast expanse of sea ice known as the Arctic sea ice, have a highly reflective surface. This means that a large portion of the incoming solar radiation is reflected back into space, preventing it from being absorbed by the Earth's surface and thereby cooling the planet. This phenomenon, called the albedo effect, helps regulate global temperature by reducing the amount of solar energy that reaches the lower latitudes.

Additionally, the seasonal growth and retreat of Arctic sea ice have a significant impact on the Earth's ocean currents and circulation patterns. During the winter months, when the Arctic experiences prolonged darkness and extremely cold temperatures, the sea ice spreads and thickens, leading to the isolation of the adjoining ocean from the atmosphere. This insulation helps promote the formation of dense, nutrient-rich water masses that sink to the depths of the ocean and contribute to global thermohaline circulation, which carries heat and nutrients around the globe.

Moreover, the Arctic's cold and relatively fresh water play a crucial role in maintaining the circulation of the North Atlantic Ocean. The melting of Greenland's ice sheet and the inflow of freshwater from melting Arctic sea ice can disrupt the density-driven sinking of water in the North Atlantic, impacting the meridional overturning circulation. This circulation, also known as the Atlantic conveyor belt, transports warm surface water to the high latitudes and returns cold, deep water southward, distributing heat and regulating the Earth's climate. Any interruptions in this process can have far-reaching consequences for global climate patterns.

Furthermore, the Arctic's position on the Earth's axis also plays a role in regulating global climate. The region experiences extreme seasonal variations in sunlight, with periods of continuous darkness during winter and continuous sunlight during summer. This difference in energy input drives temperature gradients and pressure systems, affecting atmospheric circulation patterns globally. The changes in the Arctic's climate, particularly the reduction in sea ice extent and thickness, have been linked to altered jet stream patterns, leading to more frequent and persistent weather extremes in lower latitudes, such as heatwaves, droughts, and severe storms.

Finally, the Arctic is home to vast stores of carbon in the form of permafrost and ocean sediments. The escalating temperatures in the region are causing the thawing of permafrost and the release of substantial amounts of greenhouse gases, such as carbon dioxide and methane. These emissions contribute to the amplification of global warming, further intensifying the changes occurring in the Arctic and impacting climate systems worldwide.

In conclusion, the Arctic's role in regulating global climate is of paramount importance. Its extensive ice and snow cover, the growth and retreat of sea ice, its cold and fresh water, the unique seasonal variations in sunlight, and the release of carbon from thawing permafrost all contribute to its significant influence on Earth's climate system. Understanding and assessing these processes is essential for predicting and responding to future climate change, as the interconnectedness of the Earth's climate requires a comprehensive examination of the Arctic's role.

- Vulnerability of Arctic ecosystems to climate change

The Arctic region is undergoing rapid and unprecedented changes as a result of climate change. The impact of rising global temperatures is especially pronounced in this vulnerable ecosystem, with implications for its unique and diverse plant and animal species, as well as local communities and global climate patterns. Understanding the vulnerability of Arctic ecosystems to climate change is crucial for informing conservation strategies and ensuring the long-term survival of this delicate region.

One of the main concerns for Arctic ecosystems is the loss of sea ice, which acts as a crucial habitat for many species, including polar bears, seals, and walruses. As temperatures rise, sea ice melts at an alarming rate, reducing the area and duration of ice cover. This not only limits availability of ice-dependent species' hunting grounds, but also affects their ability to reproduce, rest, and seek refuge from predators. The decline in sea ice also has repercussions for the delicate food web, as it disrupts the timing and availability of plankton growth, which impacts the entire marine ecosystem.

Another vulnerable component of Arctic ecosystems is permafrost, which refers to frozen ground that remains below 0 °C for at least two consecutive years. Permafrost covers approximately a quarter of the Northern Hemisphere, storing substantial amounts of carbon released by decaying organic matter over thousands of years. However, as temperatures rise, permafrost is no longer permanent, resulting in the thawing of frozen organic matter. This process releases large amounts of greenhouse gases, namely carbon dioxide and methane, into the atmosphere, further exacerbating global warming and contributing to a vicious cycle.

Furthermore, the loss of sea ice and warming of Arctic waters influences vital marine processes such as circulation patterns and nutrient availability. The reduction in sea ice creates a larger expanse of open water, leading to increased evaporation, which in turn contributes to changes in humidity and precipitation patterns around the globe. This disruption of the ocean-atmosphere system not only affects weather patterns but also global ocean currents, which play a major role in regulating the Earth's climate.

Human communities living in the Arctic region are also heavily dependent on natural resources affected by climate change. Indigenous people rely on subsistence hunting, fishing, and gathering as a way of life, and changing environmental conditions pose significant challenges. Diminished availability of key species, unsafe ice conditions for transportation and traditional practices, and altered migratory patterns of animals impact the livelihoods and cultural identity of these communities.

Adaptation strategies to safeguard Arctic ecosystems and the livelihoods of local communities require a multi-faceted approach. Efforts should focus on mitigating greenhouse gas emissions to slow down the pace of climate change at a global level. Localized conservation efforts can include establishing protected areas that ensure the preservation of key habitats and the protection of vulnerable species. Collaboration between indigenous peoples, scientists, and policymakers is crucial to ensure that the unique perspective and traditional knowledge of Arctic communities are incorporated into decision-making processes.

In summary, the vulnerability of Arctic ecosystems to climate change is underscored by the ongoing loss of sea ice, thawing permafrost, and the disruption of crucial marine processes. These changes have far-reaching implications for wildlife, local communities, and global climate patterns. Combating climate change and implementing effective conservation initiatives are of paramount importance to preserve the delicate Arctic ecosystem and safeguard its invaluable biodiversity.

- Summary of past and current changes in Arctic climate

The Arctic climate has experienced significant changes in the past few decades, with noticeable impacts on the environment and ecosystem. The region has been warming at a much faster rate compared to the rest of the planet, a trend that has gained momentum in recent years.

Historically, the Arctic has gone through natural climate variations, experiencing periods of cooling and warming in cycles. However, the current warming trend is occurring at an unprecedented rate, largely attributed to human-induced factors, specifically the release of greenhouse gases into the atmosphere.

Temperatures in the Arctic have risen by almost twice the global average over the past century. This rapid warming has resulted in various changes including the shrinking of the Arctic sea ice. Summer sea ice extent has diminished significantly, and the thickness of the ice has also decreased. The region now experiences more open water, leading to changes in ocean circulation patterns and disrupting various ecosystems, affecting the habitat of numerous Arctic species including polar bears, seals, and seabirds.

Another consequence of Arctic warming is the thawing of permafrost-permanently frozen ground that covers a large portion of the region. As the permafrost thaws, it releases stored carbon dioxide and methane, which are potent greenhouse gases, further exacerbating global warming. This process also poses a significant risk to infrastructure built on permafrost, such as roads, buildings, and pipelines.

Melting glaciers and ice caps in the Arctic are contributing to rising sea levels worldwide, threatening coastal communities and low-lying islands. The loss of reflective ice surfaces in the region also amplifies the feedback loop of warming, as darker surfaces absorb more sunlight compared to ice, expediting the heating of the atmosphere.

These changes in Arctic climate are not just confined to the region but have global ramifications. As sea ice continues to melt, it reduces the planet's ability to reflect solar radiation back into space, leading to further warming. Additionally, changes in ocean circulation triggered by Arctic warming can affect global weather patterns and even modify ocean currents, influencing weather events far beyond the polar region.

Efforts to mitigate and adapt to these changes are vital. Many nations, along with scientific and environmental organizations, are working towards reducing greenhouse gas emissions, promoting sustainable practices, and protecting vulnerable Arctic habitats. Understanding the past and current changes in Arctic climate is key to developing effective strategies for preserving this delicate ecosystem and minimizing the impacts of climate change on a global scale.

Chapter 4: Climate Models and Predictions

Climate change is a pressing global issue that requires comprehensive understanding and accurate predictions. Climate models play a crucial role in helping us understand the complex dynamics of the climate system and project future changes. This chapter delves into the intricacies of climate models, their development, and their applications in predicting climate scenarios.

Development of Climate Models:

Climate models are mathematical representations of the Earth's climate system. They simulate the interactions between various components, such as the atmosphere, oceans, land surfaces, and ice sheets. Over the years, considerable progress has been made in developing these models, incorporating more comprehensive physics and Earth system processes.

To begin, climate models are based on fundamental physical principles, such as the laws of thermodynamics and fluid dynamics. Through numerical approximations, these principles are translated into computational algorithms that can simulate the behavior of the climate system over time.

The Equations:

The basic equations used in climate models include the Navier-Stokes equations for fluid motion, the energy conservation equation, and the radiative transfer equations for the interactions of solar and thermal radiation with the atmosphere. These equations, along with parameterizations of sub-grid-scale processes, are solved on a grid that discretizes the Earth's surface, atmosphere, and oceans.

Modeling Components:

Climate models are composed of various modules, each representing a different component of the climate system. The atmosphere module simulates the dynamics of the atmosphere, incorporating important factors such as wind, temperature, and precipitation patterns. The ocean module accounts for the circulation patterns and thermal characteristics of the world's oceans.

Additionally, land surface modules simulate the exchange of energy, water, and carbon with the atmosphere.

Model Evaluation and Validation:

Given the complexity of climate models, accurately representing every aspect of the climate system is challenging. Therefore, model outputs need to be continually evaluated against observed climate data. Model developers compare simulated climate variables, like surface air temperature and precipitation, with real-world measurements to assess their accuracy. This process helps identify model biases and areas for improvement.

Uncertainty in Climate Models:

Climate models involve numerous uncertainties due to incomplete data, limitations in computing power, and uncertainties inherent in the mathematical representations of physical processes. Climate scientists employ ensemble modeling to account for these uncertainties. By running multiple simulations with slight differences in input parameters, researchers can assess the range of possible outcomes represented by a model.

Model Projections:

Climate models have provided valuable insights into how Earth's climate may change in response to increasing greenhouse gas concentrations. By projecting future climate scenarios, policymakers and scientists can make informed decisions and develop adaptation strategies. However, there remain uncertainties in these projections, particularly related to how human societies will evolve and respond to climate change, highlighting the importance of continued research.

⚫

CLIMATE MODELS CONSTITUTE the backbone of climate science, aiding our understanding of the past, present, and potential future of our planet's climate. Their development and application require interdisciplinary collaboration and ongoing research efforts. As these models continue to improve and incorporate new data, their predictions will become even more accurate and useful for decision-making on local, national, and global scales.

- Explanation of climate modeling techniques

Climate modeling techniques are powerful tools used by scientists to understand and predict how our climate system works, and how it may change in the future. These techniques involve complex mathematical algorithms and simulations of Earth's climate system, combining knowledge from various scientific disciplines such as physics, chemistry, biology, and geology. In this article, we will explore the different modeling techniques used to examine climate phenomena, improve our understanding of climate processes, and inform policy decisions.

One fundamental practice in climate modeling is creating General Circulation Models (GCMs). GCMs simulate Earth's climate system by dividing the globe into grid cells, which are boxes drawing on information from atmospheric and oceanic conditions. Scientists have developed a range of GCMs, each with slightly different features and levels of complexity, meant to capture different aspects of the climate system. These models use mathematical equations based on the fundamental laws of physics that describe how the atmosphere, oceans, land surface, ice, and other components interact with each other.

To represent interactions and processes occurring at smaller scales, climate modelers also employ Regional Climate Models (RCMs). RCMs focus on specific areas, such as a continent or a portion of an ocean, and employ a finer grid resolution compared to GCMs. By modeling climate processes with greater regional detail, RCMs can help assess how climate change may impact smaller-scale phenomena like local weather patterns, rainfall, and vegetation changes. The output from RCMs can be valuable for local and regional assessments, especially for policymakers and stakeholders at local levels.

While GCMs and RCMs provide essential insights into large-scale climate patterns, they typically lack fine-scale representation of physical processes. To bridge this knowledge gap, scientists also use more specialized models that zoom in on specific aspects such as the carbon cycle or ice dynamics. For instance, Earth System Models (ESMs) couple multiple models together, combining GCMs with additional modules to represent the carbon cycle, vegetation dynamics, and other components relevant for the Earth's ecological balance. Similarly, Ice Sheet Models simulate the movement of ice and help predict how ice sheets and glaciers will respond to ongoing climate change.

Climate modelers use observed and historical climate data to evaluate and validate their models against real-world conditions. They compare model output to reliable historical records of temperature, precipitation, sea-level rise, and other parameters to ensure their models are accurately capturing past climate dynamics. This process helps assess the reliability and accuracy of the modeling techniques and inform the credibility of future climate projections.

While climate modeling has improved our understanding of past and current climate trends, it has also been employed to project future climate scenarios. Scientists use modeling techniques to simulate various greenhouse gas emissions scenarios, allowing policymakers and researchers to explore the potential impacts and risks associated with different socioeconomic, policy, and technological choices. These projected scenarios help us to evaluate the potential consequences of global temperature rise, sea-level rise, changes in extreme weather events, and other climatic phenomena.

It is important to note that climate models are not crystal balls that can perfectly predict the future. Uncertainties exist in the models, making it challenging to achieve absolute accuracy. Climate models rely on assumptions, various input data sets, and simplifications of extremely complex systems. While researchers strive to include more processes and incorporate more detailed information into models, perfectly representing every aspect of the real climate system may not be possible.

Nonetheless, climate models play a crucial role in climate science and informing climate policy decisions. They provide insights into the potential outcomes of human actions, aiding in the mitigation of climate change and the development of adaptation strategies. As the scientific community continues to refine modeling techniques and improve their representations of the real climate system, these tool will continue to be invaluable resources for tackling climate change and its associated challenges.

- Analysis of existing climate models related to the Arctic

A nalysis of Existing Climate Models related to the Arctic

THE ARCTIC REGION IS experiencing rapid changes due to ongoing climate change, making it vital to develop accurate models for monitoring and predicting Arctic climatic conditions. Numerous climate models have been developed and used to investigate the complex interactions between various components of the climate system in the Arctic. This analysis aims to examine some of the commonly used climate models for their appropriateness, strengths, and limitations in simulating Arctic climatic processes.

Model 1: Community Earth System Model (CESM)

CESM is a widely used coupled climate system model that integrates the atmosphere, ocean, land, and sea ice components. It provides comprehensive representation of the Arctic climate and its feedback mechanisms. CESM outperforms its predecessors by incorporating more detailed physical representations of climate processes, such as sea ice albedo feedback, cloud-radiation feedbacks, and aerosol-cloud interactions. However, its computationally demanding nature often limits its spatiotemporal resolutions and complicates downscaling efforts for regional Arctic climate studies.

Model 2: European Centre HIRHAM Atmospheric Model (HIRHAM)

Developed by the European Centre for Medium-Range Weather Forecasts, HIRHAM focuses specifically on Arctic weather and climate. With its high spatial resolution, HIRHAM successfully captures small-scale atmospheric phenomena, including storms and localized wind patterns in the Arctic. However, limited parameterizations for sea ice dynamics and ocean-atmosphere interactions restrict its ability to simulate long-term climate changes in the region accurately.

Model 3: Community Climate System Model version 4 (CCSM4)

CCSM4 developed by the National Center for Atmospheric Research has been widely used for Arctic climate projections. It provides robust estimations of the climate variables influenced by surface processes, such as temperature, humidity, and rainfall. CCSM4's resolution, however, falls short in capturing detailed Arctic features at the regional scale due to computational constraints, resulting in uncertainties in modeling processes like the Arctic oscillation.

Model 4: Arctic System Reanalysis (ASR)

ASR is a state-of-the-art reanalysis product developed by the National Centers for Environmental Prediction in collaboration with other research institutions. It assimilates various observations from past decades into a consistent and coherent dataset, enhancing our understanding of the Arctic climate system. ASR provides a reliable representation of past climate conditions to validate other models, but it has limitations when it comes to capturing evolving conditions, making it less suitable for future projections.

⸻ ◉ ⸻

CLIMATE MODELS PLAY a crucial role in assessing and predicting the impacts of climate change in the Arctic. Each model discussed here has its strengths and limitations, along with potential uncertainties. A holistic approach that combines the expertise of multiple modeling frameworks can bridge existing gaps and provide more accurate simulations. By continuously refining these models and incorporating new scientific data, we can enhance our understanding of the Arctic climatic processes and effectively address the challenges posed by climate change in this critical region.

- Impact of these models on predictions for the future of the Arctic

The models used in predicting the future of the Arctic have had a tremendous impact on our understanding of this rapidly changing region. These models incorporate a wide range of data and variables to simulate various future scenarios, enabling scientists to make predictions about the trajectory of Arctic climate, sea ice cover, and other critical aspects. The overarching goal of these models is to provide policymakers, researchers, and the public with valuable insights into the potential environmental and socio-economic consequences of a changing Arctic.

One of the most important contributions of these models is their ability to elucidate the impacts of climate change on Arctic sea ice extent. By factoring in greenhouse gas emissions scenarios and other climate drivers, scientists have been able to project a future with significantly reduced summer ice cover in the Arctic Ocean. Estimates indicate that by the middle of the century, the Arctic could become essentially ice-free during summers, leading to significant ecological and societal consequences.

These models also offer valuable insights into the effects of warming temperatures on Arctic ecosystems. Higher temperatures are likely to trigger significant shifts in species distributions, with climate-sensitive species such as polar bears, walruses, and certain bird populations facing increased challenges to their survival. Additionally, the projections suggest that ocean acidification resulting from increased carbon dioxide concentration and changing sea-ice dynamics could have profound implications for the Arctic's fragile marine ecosystem and its productivity.

Furthermore, these models allow us to understand the potential impacts on regional weather patterns, global climate systems, and even geopolitical dynamics. For instance, as the Arctic undergoes rapid warming, the models indicate that this region could become more accessible, leading to enhanced economic activities such as shipping, resource extraction, and tourism. These newfound opportunities have prompted various nations, including the United States, Russia, Canada, and China, to reassess their Arctic policies and increase their presence in the region.

The predictive power of these models also helps policymakers and local communities prepare for the anticipated environmental challenges. For instance, the insights gained from modeling studies enable the development of effective strategies for adapting to a changing Arctic, such as constructing climate-resilient infrastructure, revising national regulations, and fostering international cooperation on environmental protection.

Nevertheless, it is crucial to acknowledge that these models are not perfect crystal balls. Variabilities in data quality, measurement uncertainties, and the sheer complexity of interconnected systems make predictions inherently uncertain. Therefore, continuous refinement of models and incorporation of new data are critical to improve our understanding of the Arctic's future. Additionally, engaging with local communities and Indigenous peoples in the development and use of these models is essential for incorporating traditional knowledge, enhancing accuracy, and ensuring that adaptations adequately address local needs.

In conclusion, the models used to predict the future of the Arctic offer important and captivating insights into the potential consequences of climate change in this fragile region. By deciphering the impacts on sea ice extent, ecosystems, weather patterns, and geopolitical dynamics, these models provide a foundation for effective policymaking, adaptation strategies, and environmental stewardship. Although the accuracy of predictions is not absolute due to inherent uncertainties, these models help us comprehend the potential future of the Arctic and the imperative of sustainable actions to mitigate the risks associated with a rapidly changing environment.

- Discussion on uncertainties and challenges in modeling Arctic climate change

Arctic climate change is a widely researched and important area of study due to its potential implications for global climate patterns and the abundance of natural resources within the region. As scientists and policymakers seek to understand and prepare for the changes occurring in the Arctic, modeling plays a crucial role in assessing and predicting the future state of the region. However, there are a few key uncertainties and challenges that need to be addressed in order to develop accurate and reliable models.

One of the major uncertainties in modeling Arctic climate change is the representation of feedback mechanisms. Feedback loops are processes in which the effects of climate change either amplify or dampen the initial change. For example, the melting of sea ice exposes the darker ocean surface, which leads to increased absorption of solar radiation and further warming of the Arctic. This positive feedback loop can have significant impacts on the rate of warming in the region. However, the strength and dynamics of these feedback mechanisms are not fully understood, making it difficult to accurately represent them in models.

Another challenge in modeling Arctic climate change is the lack of historical data for the region. The Arctic is a remote and harsh environment, making it difficult to collect long-term observational data. This limits the availability of data needed for model evaluation and validation. In addition, data gaps and inconsistencies in historical records make it challenging to accurately capture the complex dynamics of Arctic climate processes in models.

Furthermore, uncertainties in modeling arise from the simplified representation of complex physical processes. Due to the computational constraints, climate models make assumptions and parameterizations to simplify the representation of physical processes. These simplifications can introduce uncertainties in model results. For example, models may not fully capture the intricate interactions between the atmosphere, ocean, land, and sea ice layers. This can result in uncertainties in projecting future changes in Arctic climate variables such as temperature, sea ice extent, and precipitation.

Alongside model uncertainties, challenges in modeling Arctic climate change also stem from external factors. For instance, the Arctic is geopolitically influenced by a changing economic landscape and regional conflicts. These external factors can introduce additional uncertainties into modeling by affecting future emissions pathways, technological advancements, and policy decisions. Incorporating these uncertainties in models is crucial to account for the possible range of climate scenarios and improve preparedness.

To address these uncertainties and challenges, ongoing research efforts are aimed at improving the representation of feedback mechanisms, expanding observational networks, and refining parameterizations in models. Advances in satellite remote sensing and improved modeling techniques have led to increased availability of observational data and more sophisticated models. Additionally, collaborative international efforts, such as the Coupled Model Intercomparison Project (CMIP), have allowed for the inter-comparison of different models and evaluation against observations, thus reducing uncertainties.

In conclusion, while modeling Arctic climate change is an essential tool, there are several uncertainties and challenges that need to be addressed. These range from understanding and representing feedback mechanisms accurately, to improving data availability, and refining model parameterizations. Addressing these challenges is crucial for developing accurate and reliable models to aid in understanding, predicting, and mitigating the impacts of Arctic climate change.

Chapter 5: Warming Trends and Temperature Rise in the Arctic

In Chapter 5 of our research paper, we delve into an exploration of warming trends and temperature rise in the Arctic region. This chapter provides a rich and comprehensive analysis of the past, current, and projected changes in the Arctic climate.

We begin by providing a detailed background of the Arctic climate system, highlighting its unique characteristics and vulnerability to climate change. The chapter then progresses into a thorough examination of the current warming trends in the Arctic, drawing upon observational records, satellite data, and climate models.

We present a historical perspective on the temperature rise in the Arctic, discussing the instrumental temperature records dating back several decades. This temporal analysis sheds light on the steady increase in Arctic temperatures over the years and allows us to better understand the magnitude and pace of the temperature rise.

Furthermore, we explore the spatial distribution of the warming, presenting data on temperature anomalies across different Arctic regions. This analysis not only emphasizes the localized nature of the warming but also highlights the spatial variability in temperature increase, informing us of the disproportionate impact on specific areas within the Arctic.

To comprehensively examine the causes of this temperature rise, we delve into the various mechanisms and forcings at play. We discuss the role of greenhouse gas emissions, the amplification effect of the Arctic climate system, and feedback processes involved in Arctic temperature change. This discussion provides both a holistic overview as well as a more nuanced understanding of the complex factors contributing to the warming trends.

Moreover, we investigate the consequences of the rising temperatures in the Arctic, paying particular attention to ecological, environmental, and socio-economic impacts. The chapter explores how the temperature rise affects sea ice extent and thickness, permafrost stability, and the livelihoods of Arctic indigenous communities. This analysis offers insight into the vast and multifaceted implications of Arctic warming, further highlighting the urgent need for climate action.

To comprehend future climate scenarios, we present the projected temperature rise in the Arctic under different greenhouse gas emissions scenarios. This discussion utilizes state-of-the-art climate models and clearly demonstrates the potential severity of future warming in the region. Through this analysis, we aim to provide a forecast of the magnitude, duration, and spatial distribution of the temperature rise in the coming decades.

In conclusion, Chapter 5 offers a lengthy yet compelling account of the warming trends and temperature rise in the Arctic. Through its detailed examination of historical records, spatial distribution, causative factors, and projected scenarios, this chapter presents a holistic view of Arctic climate change. Its in-depth analysis and informative content make it an engrossing and enriching read for anyone interested in understanding the current and future state of the Arctic.

- Examination of historical temperature records in the Arctic

The examination of historical temperature records in the Arctic reveals a wealth of valuable information about the region's climate and its changes over time. These records, spanning several decades to even centuries, help scientists understand the past and present climate patterns, and make projections for future climate scenarios.

One of the most significant sources of historical temperature data in the Arctic comes from meteorological stations, which have been systematically measuring and recording weather patterns for decades. These stations provide crucial data on temperature variations throughout the year, including average temperatures, seasonal fluctuations, and extreme events.

Analysis of temperature records from meteorological stations has brought to light alarming trends in Arctic temperatures. Over the past century, the Arctic has experienced a much more rapid rate of warming compared to other regions of the globe. This phenomenon, known as Arctic amplification, is attributed to various factors, including feedback loops linked to the melting of ice and snow.

One of the key indicators of Arctic warming is the rise in annual average temperatures. Historical records show a steady increase in temperatures over the past century, with a particularly pronounced rise in the past few decades. This warming trend has repercussions for the ecosystem as a whole, affecting wildlife, vegetation, and oceanic patterns.

In addition to average temperatures, historical records also shed light on seasonal temperature variations. Data indicate that winter warming in the Arctic has outpaced summer warming, resulting in a narrowing of the temperature range between these two seasons. This has substantial implications for sea ice extent, as the onset and duration of the freeze-up and melting seasons are sensitive to temperature changes.

Extreme temperature events in the Arctic have also been documented through historical records. Heatwaves, which were previously rare occurrences in the region, have become more frequent and more intense in recent years. These events have significant consequences, causing accelerated ice melting, permafrost thawing, and an increased risk of wildfires.

While meteorological stations provide a valuable dataset for understanding historical temperature changes in the Arctic, they have limitations. Station density in the region is relatively sparse, particularly in remote areas, resulting in interpolation challenges. This scarcity of data in certain regions hinders a comprehensive understanding of temperature variability across the entire Arctic.

To overcome these limitations, scientists turn to other sources of historical temperature records, including ice cores and tree rings. Ice cores, obtained by drilling into ice sheets and glaciers, contain air bubbles that preserve a record of past atmospheric temperatures and composition. By measuring the isotopic composition of oxygen, scientists can estimate past temperature changes over thousands of years.

Similarly, tree rings can serve as proxies for past temperatures in the Arctic. Trees growing in the region's harsh conditions respond to temperature variations and produce annual rings that can be studied to reconstruct historical climatic conditions. This dendroclimatology approach helps expand our knowledge of temperature records beyond the instrumental period.

Collectively, the examination of historical temperature records in the Arctic reveals a region that is experiencing rapid and significant warming. These records provide unique insights into past climate variability while underlining the urgent need for action to mitigate further temperature rise and its potential consequences on the Arctic ecosystem, global weather patterns, and sea-level rise. Continuous monitoring and analysis of both past and present temperatures will be crucial to understanding the Arctic's climatic trajectory and devising effective strategies for adaptation and mitigation.

- Analysis of the accelerating warming trends in the region

The accelerating warming trends in the region have brought about significant changes in recent years. The increase in average temperatures, changing precipitation patterns, and shifts in ecosystems have become undeniable evidence of global climate change.

One of the key factors driving the accelerating warming trends is the rapid industrialization and associated increase in greenhouse gas emissions. The burning of fossil fuels, such as oil, coal, and natural gas, releases vast amounts of carbon dioxide into the atmosphere. These greenhouse gases trap heat in the Earth's atmosphere, leading to a rise in average temperatures.

In addition to industrial emissions, deforestation and urbanization also contribute to increased warming. Forests play a vital role in absorbing carbon dioxide from the atmosphere through the process of photosynthesis. However, large-scale deforestation has led to a reduction in the Earth's natural carbon sink, causing more carbon dioxide to accumulate in the atmosphere.

The consequences of these accelerating warming trends are highly concerning. The region has experienced a multitude of impacts, including rising sea levels, ocean acidification, and extreme weather events. Low-lying coastal areas are especially vulnerable to the effects of sea-level rise, which pose a significant threat to communities and infrastructure in these regions.

Precipitation patterns have also been altered, with some areas experiencing extended periods of drought, while others are struck by intense rainfall and flooding. These changes in precipitation are not only affecting agricultural crops but can also lead to water scarcity and exacerbate existing conflicts over freshwater resources.

Moreover, ecosystems are undergoing significant shifts as a result of the accelerating warming. Plant and animal species are being forced to adapt to new environmental conditions or migrate to more suitable habitats. However, many species are struggling to keep up, leading to declines in biodiversity and potential ecosystem disruptions.

To address these accelerating warming trends, a comprehensive and immediate response is needed at both the global and local levels. Governments, industries, and individuals all have a role to play in reducing greenhouse gas emissions. This can be achieved through a wide range of actions, such as transitioning to renewable energy sources, implementing energy efficiency measures, and promoting sustainable land management practices.

Adaptation strategies are also crucial, as the impacts of global warming are already being felt and will continue to affect communities and ecosystems. This includes developing resilient infrastructure, implementing sustainable water management practices, and conserving protected areas to safeguard biodiversity.

In conclusion, the analysis of the accelerating warming trends in the region reveals the urgent need for collective action to mitigate the causes and adapt to the consequences of climate change. The long-term well-being and sustainability of the region's natural systems and human populations depend on our ability to address this pressing global challenge.

- Dissection of climate feedback mechanisms intensifying Arctic warming

Dissection of Climate Feedback Mechanisms Intensifying Arctic Warming

THE ARCTIC REGION PLAYS a crucial role in Earth's climate system, acting as a key amplifier for global warming. Over the past few decades, Arctic temperatures have been rising at an alarming rate, more than over twice as fast as the global average. This trend, known as Arctic amplification, has far-reaching consequences for climatic and environmental patterns around the world. Understanding the mechanisms responsible for intensifying Arctic warming is essential for accurate climate modeling and projecting future trends. This essay delves into the complex web of climate feedback mechanisms that contribute to Arctic amplification.

I. Sea Ice-Albedo Feedback:

The sea ice-albedo feedback is central to understanding Arctic amplification and serves as a prime example of a positive feedback loop. As global temperatures rise, Arctic sea ice undergoes significant reductions in volume and extent. Reduced ice coverage reflects less sunlight back into space, which leads to further warming of the region. Higher temperatures in turn cause more ice melt and a continuation of this feedback loop. The uninterrupted decline in sea ice cover also has profound impacts on ecosystems, wildlife habitats, and indigenous communities deeply reliant on the Arctic environment.

II. Heat-Absorbing Feedback in the Oceans:

Another key factor accelerating Arctic warming is the role of the oceans. The influx of warm water into the Arctic can occur through two primary pathways. Firstly, a weakened Beaufort Gyre, driven by Arctic amplification itself, pulls in relatively warmer waters from the Atlantic and Pacific Oceans. Secondly, changes in wind patterns and atmospheric circulation can transport heat from lower-latitude regions into the Arctic. As the Arctic Ocean absorbs more heat, the increased temperature further reduces sea ice cover, reducing albedo, and amplifying warming.

III. Methane Release from Thawing Permafrost:

Arctic permafrost, vast areas of permanently frozen ground, contains significant stores of organic matter in the form of dead vegetation. As permafrost thaws due to rising temperatures, microbial decomposition increases, releasing substantial amounts of methane—a potent greenhouse gas. Methane emitted from thawing permafrost amplifies global warming by capturing more outgoing longwave radiation, further intensifying Arctic warming in a self-perpetuating feedback loop. The severity of this feedback loop is particularly concerning since amplified Arctic warming is causing accelerated permafrost degradation.

IV. Stratospheric Influence:

Under normal conditions, the Arctic stratosphere remains cold and isolated from the troposphere. However, increased Arctic temperatures can lead to rapid losses of stratospheric ozone, altering the polar vortex. This allows the transfer of high-ozone airmasses out of the stratosphere into the Arctic troposphere during winter. These stratospheric ozone-depleted airmasses induce substantial heating, further intensifying Arctic warming and influencing large-scale atmospheric circulation patterns, including the polar jet stream.

⎯⎯⎯◉⎯⎯⎯

THE DISSECTION OF CLIMATE feedback mechanisms contributing to Arctic amplification reveals an intricate web of interconnections between various Earth systems. The sea ice-albedo feedback, heat-absorbing feedback in the oceans, methane release from thawing permafrost, and stratospheric influence collectively strengthen Arctic warming. Understanding these feedback loops is pivotal for climate scientists as they project future climate scenarios. Mitigating the effects of Arctic amplification requires global efforts to reduce greenhouse gas emissions and combat climate change comprehensively. Failure to tackle this issue may lead to irreversible changes in the Arctic and have drastic consequences on global climate stability.

- Overview of impacts on wildlife, ecosystems, and indigenous communities

Overview of Impacts on Wildlife, Ecosystems, and Indigenous Communities

THE INTERACTION BETWEEN human development and the natural world has led to significant impacts on various ecosystems, wildlife populations, and indigenous communities. This article provides a detailed overview of these impacts, highlighting the intricate relationship between humans and their surrounding environment.

I. Impacts on Wildlife:

1. Fragmentation:

- Human activities such as deforestation, urbanization, and infrastructure development have led to the fragmentation of natural habitats, isolating wildlife populations and reducing gene flow.

- Fragmentation disrupts migration patterns, alters animal behavior, and leads to population declines and increased extinction risks.

2. Habitat Loss:

- Unsustainable land use practices, primarily driven by agriculture and resource extraction, cause catastrophic habitat loss for wildlife.

- Destruction of critical habitats threatens the survival of numerous species, leading to declines in biodiversity and potential ecosystem collapse.

3. Pollution:

- Pollution from industrial runoff, chemical pesticides, and plastics adversely affects wildlife populations.

- Accumulation of toxins in the environment can harm organisms directly, disrupt food webs, and lead to population declines or local extinctions.

4. Climate Change:

- Rapid climate change caused by human activities, such as carbon emissions, alters habitats and disrupts ecosystems.

- Shifts in temperature and precipitation patterns affect wildlife migration, reproductive cycles, and availability of essential resources, adversely impacting wildlife populations.

II. Impacts on Ecosystems:

1. Biodiversity Loss:

- Constant human intervention in natural ecosystems results in the decline of biodiversity.

- Ecosystems with reduced species diversity face greater instability, susceptibility to invasive species, and decreased resilience to environmental changes.

2. Disruption of Food Chains:

- Destruction of habitat and overexploitation of key species disrupts food chains.

- The disappearance of keystone species can trigger cascading effects, leading to imbalances throughout the ecosystem and potentially compromising its overall structure and function.

3. Introduction of Invasive Species:

- Human activities, such as global trade and transportation, inadvertently introduce invasive species into new environments.

- Invasive species can outcompete native flora and fauna, negatively affecting ecosystem processes and driving native species towards extinction.

III. Impacts on Indigenous Communities:

1. Cultural Disruption:

- The encroachment of economic development into indigenous territories disrupts traditional cultural practices and spiritual connections with the land.

- Loss of cultural heritage erodes identity, community cohesion, and resilience.

2. Loss of Livelihood:

- Indigenous communities heavily depend on natural resources for sustenance, livelihoods, and economic activities.

- Degradation of ecosystems and wildlife populations negatively impacts indigenous livelihoods, often leading to poverty and food insecurity.

3. Socioeconomic Inequality:

- Indigenous communities often face socioeconomic and political marginalization, making them more vulnerable to the impacts of development.

- Limited access to resources, healthcare, and education exacerbates their struggle to adapt and cope with environmental changes.

45

UNDERSTANDING THE BROAD-ranging impacts of human activities on wildlife, ecosystems, and indigenous communities is crucial for sustainable development. Balancing economic progress with the conservation of natural resources and indigenous rights becomes essential in mitigating and preventing further harm to our environment and its interconnected components.

Chapter 6: Melting Ice and Rising Sea Levels

In this chapter, we delve into the fascinating and increasingly concerning phenomenon of melting ice and rising sea levels. The Earth's climate is changing, and the consequences are far-reaching. This chapter will explore the causes and effects of melting ice and how it contributes to the rise in sea levels. Additionally, we will discuss the potential impacts on coastal communities and the wider implications for the planet.

The Causes of Melting Ice:

Global warming is the primary driver behind melting ice. The increase in greenhouse gas emissions, such as carbon dioxide, has created a greenhouse effect, trapping heat and raising temperatures worldwide. This elevated temperature leads to the melting of ice in both polar regions and mountainous regions around the globe.

The Arctic region is particularly susceptible to global warming. The Greenland Ice Sheet, for example, is steadily losing mass due to rising temperatures. The balance between ice accumulation through snowfall and ice loss through melting can tip in favor of the latter. This leads to an overall reduction in ice volume and a net contribution to rising sea levels.

In Antarctica, warming oceans are causing the disintegration of ice shelves. These vast floating extensions of glaciers act as buttresses, holding back immense ice masses on land. As they crumble into the sea, more land-based ice moves toward the ocean, adding to the overall sea level rise.

Effects on Sea Levels:

The consequences of melting ice are most evident in the observed rise in sea levels globally. As large ice sheets or glaciers melt and flow into the oceans, the volume of water increases, resulting in a rise in sea levels. This poses unprecedented risks to coastal communities, low-lying islands, and fragile ecosystems.

According to the Intergovernmental Panel on Climate Change (IPCC), sea levels have risen at an average rate of 3.6 millimeters per year over the past decade. The rate is projected to accelerate as warming continues. By the end of this century, sea levels could rise by up to a meter, displacing millions of people and flooding extensive areas of land.

Impacts on Coastal Communities:

Coastal cities around the world are already experiencing the first signs of rising sea levels. Increased flooding events, particularly during high tides and storms, are becoming more frequent and severe. Infrastructure such as roads, homes, and businesses located in coastal zones could face unprecedented damage.

Vulnerable countries like Bangladesh, the Maldives, and numerous Pacific island nations are especially at risk. These regions often lack the resources to implement extensive coastal defenses or relocate communities. Climate-induced migration may become a reality as people are forced to abandon their homes in search of safer ground.

Interconnected Effects on Ecosystems and Climate:

The melting of ice and rising sea levels have far-reaching impacts beyond coastal populations. As saline waters infiltrate freshwater systems, vital habitats such as wetlands, mangroves, and estuaries are imbalanced. This disruption affects species that depend on these ecosystems for survival, including migratory birds, fish, and mammals.

Additionally, the influx of freshwater due to melting ice can alter ocean currents and temperature patterns. These changes can disrupt global weather systems, influencing regional climate conditions. This interconnectedness underscores the urgent need to mitigate the effects of melting ice and address the root causes of climate change.

<hr>

CHAPTER 6 HAS PROVIDED an in-depth exploration of melting ice and rising sea levels. The fossil fuel-driven climate crisis is threatening the delicate balance of our planet's ice sheets, resulting in a continuous rise in global sea levels. The impacts on coastal communities, ecosystems, and climate patterns demand immediate action.

By understanding the causes and consequences of melting ice, we can work towards sustainable solutions, such as reducing greenhouse gas emissions and transitioning to renewable energy sources. Melting ice and rising sea levels sound the alarm for us to address the climate crisis with urgency, responsibility, and a shared commitment to safeguard our future.

- Overview of sea ice decline in the Arctic and associated consequences

The Arctic sea ice has experienced a significant decline in recent decades due to the effects of climate change. This decline has far-reaching consequences for the region's ecosystem, wildlife species, indigenous communities, global climate patterns, and even the global economy.

The Arctic region is home to a unique and diverse ecosystem that thrives in the cold and icy conditions. The sea ice provides a critical habitat for various species, including polar bears, walruses, seals, and numerous bird species. It serves as a hunting ground, mating site, and resting place for these marine animals. However, as the sea ice diminishes, their habitat is drastically altered, posing a serious threat to their survival.

Polar bears, for instance, heavily depend on sea ice as a platform for hunting seals, their primary food source. As the ice retreats, polar bears are forced to swim longer distances to find food, leading to increased exhaustion and in some cases, death due to drowning or starvation. The decline in polar bear populations has far-reaching consequences not only for the bears themselves but also for the entire Arctic ecosystem, as they are considered a keystone species.

Furthermore, the loss of sea ice alters the feeding patterns and migratory routes of other marine species. For example, the Arctic cod, a key prey species for many Arctic predators, relies on sea ice edges for shelter and foraging. With diminishing ice cover, the availability of food and suitable habitat declines, leading to a potential disruption of food webs and the potential decline of certain fish populations.

In addition to its biological impacts, the decline of Arctic sea ice has global consequences. Sea ice helps regulate global temperature by reflecting a large amount of solar radiation back into space. With less ice cover, more sunlight is absorbed by the darker ocean surface, leading to increased warming. This, in turn, accelerates the rate of melting and contributes to the overall rise in global temperatures. The Arctic is considered a key region in the Earth's climate system, and any changes in its ice cover directly impact the planet's climate patterns.

Indigenous communities, such as the Inuit and other Arctic peoples, have historically relied on sea ice for their way of life. It has provided them with a means of transportation, hunting, and cultural activities. The decline of sea ice disrupts these traditional practices, posing a threat to their cultural heritage and altering their way of life. It also raises concerns about their food security, as their traditional food sources, such as seals and other marine mammals, become harder to reach and hunt.

From an economic standpoint, the decline in Arctic sea ice has generated new opportunities for resource development, shipping routes, and tourism. The receding ice cover has made previously inaccessible areas more accessible for oil and gas exploration, mineral extraction, and fishing. Additionally, the opening of new shipping routes, such as the Northwest Passage, can significantly reduce shipping distances and costs. However, these economic prospects come with environmental risks, including potential oil spills, increased ship traffic, and disturbance of fragile ecosystems.

To mitigate the impacts of sea ice decline in the Arctic, it is crucial to address the root cause of the problem, which is greenhouse gas emissions leading to climate change. International efforts to reduce emissions and shift to renewable energy sources are essential to slow down and potentially reverse the decline in Arctic sea ice. Additionally, collaboration between scientists, policymakers, and local communities is necessary to develop adaptation strategies that will support the resilience of the Arctic ecosystem and the communities directly affected by the changes.

In summary, the Arctic sea ice has experienced a rapid decline in recent decades, which has serious ecological, cultural, economic, and global repercussions. Understanding the complex interactions and consequences of this decline is vital to mitigate its impacts and preserve the Arctic ecosystem and the communities that depend on it.

- Analysis of decreased ice coverage and ice thickness

Analysis of Decreased Ice Coverage and Ice Thickness

THE EARTH'S CLIMATE is constantly changing, and one significant indication of this change is the decrease in ice coverage and ice thickness in various regions of the world. This analysis aims to explore the reasons behind this trend, as well as the implications for the Earth's environment and ecosystems.

Decreasing Ice Coverage:

1. Climate Change:

One of the primary drivers behind the decreased ice coverage is climate change. Rising global temperatures caused by the increase in greenhouse gas emissions have led to the melting of ice in the Arctic, Antarctic, and various glaciers worldwide. This warming trend disrupts the equilibrium of the cryosphere and accelerates ice melting.

2. Feedback Loops:

As ice cover decreases, more sunlight is absorbed by the Earth's surface instead of being reflected back into space. This creates a positive feedback loop, where increasing temperatures lead to more ice melt and more heat absorption, further intensifying the warming effect.

3. Ocean Currents and Wind Patterns:

Changes in ocean currents and wind patterns can also contribute to decreased ice coverage. These natural forces can transport warmer water towards the poles, accelerating ice melting. Additionally, altered wind patterns can affect sea ice formation and break-up.

Implications of Decreased Ice Coverage:

1. Ecological Consequences:

The decrease in ice coverage negatively impacts numerous species that depend on ice for survival. Polar bears, seals, and walruses, for example, rely on sea ice as hunting and breeding grounds. A decline in ice coverage can lead to a loss of habitat and reduced prey availability, potentially driving these species towards extinction.

2. Rising Sea Levels:

As ice on land, such as glaciers and ice sheets, melts and drains into the sea, it contributes to rising sea levels. This can result in coastal erosion, increased flooding events, and the relocation of coastal populations and infrastructure.

Decreasing Ice Thickness:

1. Warmer Ocean Waters:

The increased flow of warmer ocean waters towards the polar regions contributes to the thinning of both sea and glacial ice. The heated waters erode the underneath of the ice, causing it to become less stable and ultimately leading to its decline.

2. Reduced Snowfall:

In many regions, decreased winter precipitation and increased rain instead of snowfall result in reduced ice thickness. Snowpack plays a critical role in insulating the ice from warmth, and without it, the ice is more susceptible to melt and thinning.

Implications of Decreased Ice Thickness:

1. Weakening Infrastructure:

Reduced ice thickness can pose a threat to infrastructure built on or near ice-covered regions. For example, communities that rely on ice roads or icebergs as platforms for drilling face increased risks as the ice becomes thinner and more unpredictable.

2. Impacts on Fishing and Shipping:

Thinning ice can make shipping routes more accessible in certain regions, leading to an increase in marine traffic. However, it can also make these areas dangerous and prone to accidents due to the fragile nature of the ice. Furthermore, decreased ice cover can impact fish populations, disrupting the livelihoods of those who rely on ice-associated fishing.

THE ANALYSIS OF DECREASED ice coverage and ice thickness reveals a complex interplay of climate change, feedback loops, ocean currents, and wind patterns. The implications of these trends are far-reaching, including ecological consequences, rising sea levels, weaker infrastructure, and impacts on fishing and shipping. To address these challenges, concerted efforts towards mitigating climate change are necessary, along with preserving and restoring the integrity of Earth's icy regions.

- Exploration of the implications for maritime transportation and resource exploration

Maritime transportation and resource exploration have always played a significant role in human history and continue to shape our societies today. The vastness of the world's oceans offers various opportunities for trade, travel, and the extraction of valuable resources. With technological advancements, the implications of maritime transportation and resource exploration have expanded in both positive and negative ways. This article will explore some of these implications.

One of the most immediate benefits of maritime transportation is the facilitation of global trade. Shipping goods over water is generally cheaper, faster, and more environmentally friendly compared to land-based transportation. As a result, maritime transportation enables the exchange of goods and services between countries, fostering economic growth, and empowering nations. The containerization revolution of the mid-20th century further propelled this growth by standardizing shipping practices and reducing logistics costs.

Furthermore, maritime transportation also contributes to interconnectivity and cultural exchange. Ships serve as vessels not just for goods, but also for people. From luxury cruises to commercial vessels, ships have helped shape our understanding of the world by connecting different cultures and facilitating tourism. Moreover, maritime transportation enables the movement of labor and professionals across continents, leading to the sharing of knowledge, expertise, and diverse perspectives.

However, the impacts of maritime transportation are not limited to economics and culture. There are also significant implications for resource exploration, particularly in the context of offshore drilling and deep-sea mining. As land-based resources become scarcer and more costly to acquire, the search for minerals, oil, and gas has turned to the world's oceans. The exploitation of these resources provides countries with new economic opportunities but also raises environmental concerns.

Offshore drilling for hydrocarbons carries various risks, including oil spills and pollution. Accidental spills, demonstrated by events like the Deepwater Horizon disaster in 2010, can have catastrophic consequences on marine ecosystems, wildlife, and local economies. Moreover, the extraction of fossil fuels deep below the seabed contributes to greenhouse gas emissions, exacerbating climate change.

Deep-sea mining, the exploration and extraction of minerals from the ocean floor, also presents environmental challenges. The deposits targeted for extraction are often located within unique and sensitive ecosystems, such as hydrothermal vents and cold-water coral reefs. Disrupting these ecosystems can lead to irreversible damage and the loss of biodiversity. Additionally, the process of extraction itself produces sediment plumes that can harm surrounding marine life.

Despite these concerns, maritime transportation and resource exploration can also lead to technological advancements and innovative solutions. The challenges associated with sustainable resource extraction have spurred research into cleaner technologies and practices. For example, offshore wind farms have gained traction as a renewable energy source, potentially reducing reliance on fossil fuel extraction. Likewise, advancements in underwater robotic technology have enabled better monitoring of deep-sea ecosystems, facilitating more informed decision-making in resource exploration and conservation.

In conclusion, the implications of maritime transportation and resource exploration are multi-faceted. The benefits of connecting nations, enabling global trade, and fostering cultural exchange are significant. However, the negative impacts such as oil spills, habitat destruction, and greenhouse gas emissions cannot be overlooked. As we strive for sustainable development, striking a balance between the economic benefits and environmental consequences will be vital. It is crucial to promote responsible practices, invest in research and development of clean technologies, and prioritize the long-term health of our oceans and the planet.

- Examination of the impacts of sea-level rise on coastal communities globally

Sea-level rise is a pressing issue that has global implications, particularly for the millions of people living in coastal communities. As the Earth's climate changes, the rate of sea-level rise is accelerating, largely due to the melting of glaciers and ice caps. This phenomenon not only poses significant threats to vulnerable coastal ecosystems but also has far-reaching socio-economic consequences.

Coastal communities across the globe are at the forefront of these impacts. They face increased risks of flooding, coastal erosion, and storm surges, putting lives and livelihoods in jeopardy. In densely populated areas such as cities and low-lying islands, the consequences of sea-level rise become even more pronounced.

One major concern relates to the flooding of coastal areas. With rising sea levels, regular high tides can inundate coastal regions that would previously have remained dry. This not only affects residential areas but can also contaminate freshwater sources and damage critical infrastructure such as roads, power plants, and wastewater treatment facilities. In some cases, entire communities may be displaced or forced to relocate due to the loss of habitable land.

Coastal erosion is another significant consequence of sea-level rise. As the shoreline retreats, beaches and cliffs are constantly eroded, leading to the loss of valuable land. This is especially problematic for coastal communities that heavily rely on tourism or agriculture as a source of income. In addition to financial losses, erosion can also disrupt ecosystems, including coral reefs and mangroves, which serve as natural barriers against storms and provide habitat for various species.

Increased storm surges are yet another consequence of higher sea levels. When storms occur, the higher baseline of the sea can exacerbate the destructive power of these events. The combination of elevated sea levels and powerful storm surges can lead to widespread flooding, destruction of homes, and loss of human life.

While the impacts of sea-level rise are indeed concerning, there are strategies that can be implemented to minimize the damages. One approach is to improve coastal defenses and infrastructure. This includes constructing sea walls, dykes, and levees to protect vulnerable areas from flooding and erosion. In addition, nature-based solutions, such as restoring and creating wetlands and dunes, can serve as effective defense mechanisms by acting as buffers against storm surges.

Community planning and adaptation are also crucial in dealing with sea-level rise. Governments and local authorities need to consider rising sea levels in land-use planning and zoning policies, ensuring that critical infrastructure and residential areas are built in locations that are less prone to flooding and erosion. Managed relocation may become necessary in some cases, wherein communities are moved to safer, higher ground to protect lives and livelihoods.

International cooperation is equally vital in addressing the global impacts of sea-level rise. Sharing expertise, technologies, and financial resources can assist developing countries in implementing adequate adaptation and mitigation strategies. Furthermore, reducing greenhouse gas emissions by transitioning to cleaner energy sources is an essential step in mitigating further sea-level rise and averting catastrophic consequences for coastal communities worldwide.

In conclusion, sea-level rise poses significant challenges to coastal communities globally. The threats of flooding, erosion, and storm surges are all accentuated by the advancing pace of sea-level rise. However, with comprehensive planning, resilient infrastructure, and international cooperation, the impacts of sea-level rise can be mitigated, reducing the vulnerability of coastal communities and ensuring a safer and more sustainable future.

Chapter 7: Changing Ecosystems and Biodiversity Loss

In this chapter, we will delve into the complex issue of changing ecosystems and the alarming rate of biodiversity loss. Over the years, human activities have drastically transformed natural landscapes, leading to a multitude of ecological consequences. From habitat destruction to the introduction of invasive species, these changes have had a profound impact on the delicate balance of ecosystems, resulting in the loss of countless species and overall biodiversity.

Understanding Ecosystems:

Before we discuss the changes taking place in ecosystems, it is important to first understand what an ecosystem entails. An ecosystem can be defined as a community of living organisms, together with their physical environment, functioning as a interconnected and interdependent system. These systems showcase a high level of resilience, able to adapt to certain changes in conditions. However, the vast alterations caused by human activities have outrun the ability of many ecosystems to adapt.

Habitat Destruction:

One of the primary causes of ecosystem changes and biodiversity loss is habitat destruction. Rapid urbanization, industrialization, and agricultural expansion have led to the destruction and fragmentation of natural habitats worldwide. Forests are being cleared for agriculture, wetlands are drained for development, and coral reefs are being destroyed due to climate change. These alterations in habitat structure profoundly impact the organisms that rely on specific environments, forcing them into smaller and isolated patches or displacing them entirely.

Invasive Species:

Another contributing factor to changing ecosystems is the introduction of invasive species. These are non-native organisms that establish themselves in a new environment and outcompete the native species for resources. Invasive species can wreak havoc on ecosystems since the local residents may not have evolved sufficient defenses against them. As a result, they can cause declines in native species populations, leading to a reduction in biodiversity.

Pollution and Climate Change:

Pollution and climate change have also played a significant role in ecosystem changes and biodiversity loss. From industrial pollution to the improper disposal of waste, human activities have released countless toxic substances into ecosystems. These pollutants not only harm individual organisms directly but also disrupt the delicate balance of ecosystems. Additionally, climate change, largely driven by human-induced greenhouse gas emissions, is causing shifts in temperature and precipitation patterns, impacting the availability of resources for many species and resulting in their decline or displacement.

Biodiversity Loss and Its Consequences:

The rampant changes taking place in ecosystems have resulted in a severe loss of biodiversity, known as the sixth mass extinction. Species are disappearing at an alarming rate, and ecosystems are losing their functionality due to reduced ecological interactions. Biodiversity loss has wide-ranging consequences, including the disruption of ecosystem services, such as pollination and nutrient cycling, and the potential loss of invaluable genetic resources that could offer solutions for future challenges.

Conservation Efforts:

Addressing the challenges discussed in this chapter requires robust conservation efforts. Protecting and restoring natural habitats, implementing policies to prevent the introduction of invasive species, and reducing pollution and greenhouse gas emissions are some of the strategies that can help mitigate ecosystem changes and biodiversity loss. Collaboration between governments, scientists, and local communities is crucial to developing and implementing effective conservation measures.

⸺⸺◉⸺⸺

IN THIS CHAPTER, WE have explored the intricate web of changing ecosystems and the dire consequences of biodiversity loss. Recognizing the importance of biodiversity and understanding the drivers behind ecosystem changes is essential. By taking collective action and implementing necessary conservation measures, we can hope to preserve the biological diversity that sustains our planet and ensures a flourishing future for all species.

- Implications of climate change on Arctic flora and fauna

Climate change has become an increasingly urgent global issue, with the potential to affect ecosystems and species around the world. One region that is particularly vulnerable to the impacts of climate change is the Arctic. The Arctic is home to a unique and diverse array of flora and fauna, including polar bears, reindeer, and various plant species specially adapted to the extreme cold. However, the rapid warming of the Arctic due to climate change poses significant challenges to the survival and sustainability of these fragile ecosystems.

One of the most notable impacts of climate change on Arctic flora and fauna is the loss of sea ice. Sea ice serves as an essential habitat for many species, including polar bears, seals, and walruses. It provides a platform for resting, hunting, and breeding, and its decline threatens the survival of these animals. As the Arctic warms, the extent and duration of sea ice melt increases, forcing animals to travel longer distances in search of suitable ice platforms, resulting in decreased access to food and increased mortality rates.

Additionally, melting sea ice opens up new shipping routes and allows for increased human activities, such as oil and gas exploration and fishing. These activities further exacerbate the pressure on Arctic species, as they introduce noise, pollution, and the risk of oil spills. Increased shipping activities can also introduce invasive species into the region, which can disrupt fragile ecosystems and outcompete native species for resources.

As climate change alters the fundamental features of Arctic habitats, it also impacts the plant life that has adapted to survive in this harsh environment. Arctic vegetation plays a vital role in carbon sequestration and as a food source for herbivores, such as reindeer and musk oxen. However, as the Arctic warms, plant species face numerous challenges, including increased competition from invasive species and changing soil conditions.

Warmer temperatures also allow for the expansion of shrubs and trees into areas that were once dominated by tundra vegetation. While this may seem like a positive change, as the increased plant biomass can potentially sequester more carbon, it can also have negative consequences. The encroachment of shrubs and trees into tundra ecosystems decreases habitat availability for certain species, disrupts migratory patterns, and alters the availability and distribution of food resources.

Furthermore, changes in precipitation patterns, such as an increase in rainfall and a decrease in snow cover, can lead to changes in vegetation composition and productivity. Some Arctic plants have adapted to rely on the insulating properties of snow during the cold winter months. With reduced snow cover, these plants are exposed to colder temperatures and have a lower chance of survival. Additionally, increased rainfall can lead to nutrient leaching from the soil, further impacting plant growth and survival.

Overall, the implications of climate change on Arctic flora and fauna are profound and far-reaching. Loss of sea ice, changes in vegetation composition, and alterations in precipitation patterns all contribute to the disruption of fragile Arctic ecosystems. These changes threaten the survival of numerous Arctic species, from iconic polar bears to vital plant communities. Addressing climate change and implementing mitigation and adaptation strategies is crucial to preserving the delicate balance of the Arctic and ensuring the continued existence of its unique flora and fauna.

- Analysis of key species affected by warming, such as polar bears and walruses

nalysis of Key Species Affected by Warming: A Look into Polar Bears and Walruses

GLOBAL WARMING AND its subsequent impact on wildlife have become key concerns for both scientists and conservationists worldwide. Rising temperatures and changing ecosystems are posing serious threats to various species, resulting in drastic declines in their populations. Among the most iconic species affected by warming are polar bears and walruses. In this analysis, we will delve into the ecological importance of these species, examine how warming affects their survival, and discuss the broader implications for their respective ecosystems.

1. Polar Bears:

Polar bears are unmistakably associated with the Arctic region, captivating people's imaginations due to their stunning appearance and ecological significance. As apex predators, these bears play a crucial role by regulating marine mammal populations and maintaining the overall balance of the Arctic ecosystem.

- Declining sea ice: Polar bears heavily rely on floating sea ice as their primary platform for hunting seals, a vital food source. However, the melting Arctic ice due to climate change has led to reduced sea ice cover during crucial hunting periods. Consequently, polar bears experience longer fasting periods, reduced body condition, and lower cub survival rates.

- Habitat loss: With diminished sea ice, polar bears are forced to travel longer distances, decreasing their access to prey and increasing their chances of encountering human settlements. This can lead to increased conflicts between humans and bears. Moreover, reduced access to denning areas also hampers the reproductive success of pregnant females, further threatening the survival of polar bear populations.

2. Walruses:

Known for their impressive tusks and unique adaptations, walruses are integral components of the Arctic and sub-Arctic environments. They serve as ecosystem engineers and provide an essential link in the marine food web.

- Ice-dependent foraging: Walruses primarily forage on shallow water benthic organisms, such as clams and snails. They typically rest on sea ice between feedings. However, the drastic loss of sea ice has forced walruses to switch to alternative resting sites on land, leading to overcrowding and increased mortality rates due to potential stampedes.

- Changes in prey availability: Warming waters are altering the Arctic's ocean dynamics, potentially impacting the distribution and abundance of walrus prey species. Disruptions in food availability may lead to decreased body condition, reproductive success, and overall population decline for walruses.

Broader Implications:

The impacts of global warming on polar bears and walruses are not limited to their immediate survival. The loss of these keystone species can trigger negative cascading effects throughout their respective ecosystems:

- Trophic disruptions: Without polar bears, the balance in the Arctic food web would be disrupted, potentially leading to overpopulation of certain marine mammal species and consequent declines in their prey populations. This domino effect may result in far-reaching consequences on the overall structure and functioning of the Arctic marine ecosystem.

- Loss of cultural heritage: Indigenous communities, especially those in polar regions, have deep cultural ties and traditional knowledge associated with both polar bears and walruses. The loss of these species would have significant cultural and spiritual ramifications, affecting their way of life and heritage.

⚯

THE ANALYSIS OF KEY species affected by warming, particularly polar bears and walruses, highlights the urgent need for comprehensive global climate action. Protecting these iconic species not only safeguards individual species but also ensures the preservation of entire ecosystems and the unique cultural heritage present in affected regions. By addressing the root causes of global warming and implementing adaptive conservation measures, we can preserve the majestic polar bears and magnificent walruses for future generations to admire and cherish.

- Overview of altered migration patterns and ecosystem shifts

In recent years, there has been a growing body of evidence suggesting that alterations in migration patterns and ecosystem shifts are increasingly occurring worldwide. These changes are largely attributed to human-induced factors such as climate change, habitat destruction, and pollution. Understanding these alterations is crucial for scientists, policymakers, and conservationists in order to effectively manage and mitigate their impacts on both natural systems and human communities.

Migration patterns, which are the regular movements of animals from one geographic location to another, have been found to be highly influenced by environmental factors. Many organisms, including birds, fish, insects, and even some mammals, depend on seasonal migration for various reasons such as breeding, foraging, and finding suitable habitats. However, as climate change alters the natural cycles of temperature, rainfall, and food availability, these organisms are being forced to adjust their migration patterns. For example, rising temperatures may cause some birds to migrate earlier or delay their departure, while altered rainfall patterns can impact the availability and quality of food sources along their migratory routes.

Additionally, ecosystem shifts have also been observed in various regions around the world. Ecosystems are dynamic and interconnected networks of plants, animals, and microorganisms that rely on each other for survival. However, when key species within an ecosystem are disrupted, it can trigger a chain reaction that alters its overall structure and functioning. For example, the disappearance of pollinators like bees and butterflies can disrupt the reproductive cycles of many plants, ultimately affecting food production and ecological balance. Similarly, the introduction of invasive species can outcompete native species for resources, leading to changes in species abundance and distribution.

These altered migration patterns and ecosystem shifts have far-reaching implications for both wildlife and human communities. Environmental disruptions can impact the availability of resources, including food, water, and shelter, thereby affecting the livelihoods and well-being of local populations. Moreover, as animals migrate to new areas in search of suitable habitats, conflicts can emerge with existing human settlements, leading to issues related to land use, human-wildlife interactions, and conservation practices.

Understanding these patterns and shifts is a complex and ongoing process requiring interdisciplinary research approaches. Scientists and researchers are constantly gathering data on migration patterns through the use of tracking devices, such as satellite tags and radio transmitters. Similarly, the analysis of historical records, biological surveys, and remote sensing data can provide insights into changes occurring within different ecosystems.

Efforts to mitigate the negative impacts of altered migration patterns and ecosystem shifts are diverse and multidimensional. Conservation organizations and governments are now focusing on protected area management and restoration initiatives, aiming to create wildlife corridors and buffer zones to support migratory species. Additionally, public awareness campaigns and sustainable land-use practices are important in minimizing different stressors on ecosystems and contributing to their overall resilience.

In conclusion, the alterations in migration patterns and ecosystem shifts are significant challenges that stem from human-induced factors such as climate change, habitat destruction, and pollution. The impacts of these changes are wide-ranging, affecting both wildlife and human communities. Understanding these patterns is essential for effective conservation and management practices, and mitigation efforts should strive to ensure the long-term survival and health of both natural systems and human societies.

- Discussion on the potential loss of biodiversity in the Arctic

The potential loss of biodiversity in the Arctic is a pressing issue that needs to be addressed. The region is home to many unique and diverse species, making it a crucial component of the overall global biodiversity.

One of the major factors contributing to the potential loss of biodiversity is climate change. The Arctic is already experiencing faster and more significant changes in temperature and weather patterns compared to other regions. The melting of sea ice and ice caps, in particular, poses a significant threat to many species that depend on these habitats for survival.

Polar bears, for example, rely heavily on sea ice for hunting seals, their primary prey. As the ice melts, polar bears are forced to swim longer distances, leading to increased energy expenditure and, ultimately, a decline in their population. In addition to polar bears, several other species, such as walruses, narwhals, and ringed seals, also heavily depend on sea ice for their survival. The loss of their habitat due to melting ice is putting these species at risk of extinction.

Another factor contributing to the loss of biodiversity in the Arctic is overfishing. As the region becomes more accessible due to receding ice, commercial fishing operations are expanding. This, coupled with the lack of comprehensive regulations, poses a threat to fish populations and disrupts the delicate balance of the ecosystem. Overfishing can result in the depletion of certain fish species, leading to cascading effects on the entire food chain.

Oil and gas exploration in the Arctic also present significant threats to biodiversity. The extraction of fossil fuels not only contributes to greenhouse gas emissions but also leads to habitat destruction and pollution. Oil spills, for instance, can have devastating consequences for marine life, as seen in the Deepwater Horizon disaster in 2010. Additionally, the seismic activities associated with oil and gas exploration can disturb and displace wildlife, further impacting biodiversity in the region.

Invasive species are also a concern. As the Arctic warms, certain species that are not native to the region, such as pests, weeds, and bacteria, are finding it easier to survive and thrive. These non-native species can outcompete and displace native species, further reducing biodiversity and altering the delicate balance of the ecosystem.

The loss of biodiversity in the Arctic has far-reaching implications, not only for the region itself but also for the entire planet. The Arctic plays a crucial role in regulating global climate patterns, and any disruptions to the ecosystem have the potential to have profound effects worldwide. Furthermore, the cultural heritage of indigenous peoples who rely on the region for sustenance and way of life is also at risk.

To address the potential loss of biodiversity in the Arctic, international cooperation is essential. Governments, scientists, NGOs, and local communities must work together to develop and implement effective conservation strategies. These strategies should not only focus on mitigating climate change but also on creating protected areas, enforcing fishing regulations, conducting further research on the impacts of invasive species, and ensuring responsible and sustainable resource extraction. Additionally, efforts should be made to involve and respect the traditional knowledge of indigenous peoples, who have lived sustainably in the Arctic for centuries.

In conclusion, the loss of biodiversity in the Arctic is an urgent issue that requires immediate attention. Climate change, overfishing, oil and gas exploration, and invasive species are contributing to the decline of species and threatens the delicate ecosystem of the region. It is crucial that collective efforts are made to mitigate these threats and protect the Arctic's unique and valuable biodiversity. Only through global cooperation and sustainable practices can we hope to preserve this vital ecosystem for future generations.

Chapter 8: Socioeconomic Impacts of Arctic Warming

The Arctic region has been experiencing accelerated warming, with temperatures rising at twice the global average. These changes have far-reaching implications for the socio-economic well-being of both the indigenous communities and non-indigenous people living in the Arctic. This chapter aims to provide an in-depth analysis of the socioeconomic impacts resulting from Arctic warming, shedding light on various interconnected factors.

1. Loss of infrastructure:

The warming Arctic is leading to the loss of crucial infrastructure such as roads, buildings, and ports that were designed to withstand colder conditions. As permafrost thaws, the ground becomes unstable, leading to the sinking and damage of infrastructure. These losses significantly impact economic activities and disrupt the provision of crucial services such as healthcare and education.

2. Disruptions to traditional livelihoods:

The traditional livelihoods of indigenous communities in the Arctic, such as hunting, fishing, and reindeer herding, are deeply intertwined with the stability and predictability of sea ice and other natural systems. Arctic warming is disrupting these systems, leading to reduced access to resources and a decline in the primary means of subsistence for indigenous populations. This not only affects their cultural integrity but also creates economic vulnerabilities.

3. Increased economic opportunities:

Arctic warming is also presenting new economic opportunities, particularly in sectors such as resource extraction, shipping, and tourism. As the ice cover decreases, mineral and energy resources such as oil and gas become more accessible. This has led to increased exploration and exploitation activities, which have the potential for creating employment and generating revenue. However, the sustainability and inclusiveness of these economic opportunities are still subjects of debate.

4. Health impacts:

Arctic warming has direct and indirect health impacts on local communities. Rising temperatures exacerbate the spread of infectious diseases, with melting permafrost potentially releasing ancient pathogens. Changes in food availability also impact nutrition, especially for indigenous peoples who rely heavily on traditional foods. Additionally, increased coastal erosion and the displacement of communities bring with them mental health challenges.

5. Cultural heritage and identity:

Indigenous cultures in the Arctic are deeply rooted in the natural environment and traditional practices. The loss of sea ice and other natural systems, as well as the migration and adaptation of species, affects the cultural heritage and identity of these communities. Indigenous knowledge, closely tied to the Arctic's ecological dynamics, could also be lost as younger generations are less connected to their traditional lands and practices.

6. Geopolitical implications:

The socio-economic impacts of Arctic warming extend beyond the local and regional scale. As the Arctic opens up for easier navigation and increased resource extraction, geopolitical tensions and competition among states and stakeholders rise. Issues related to territorial claims, resource exploitation, and economic influence gain prominence. The changing dynamics in the Arctic have larger implications for global politics, security, and trade.

⸻⊙⸻

ARCTIC WARMING HAS wide-ranging socioeconomic impacts that need to be carefully understood and addressed. The loss of infrastructure, disruptions to traditional livelihoods, health impacts, changing economic opportunities, cultural shifts, and geopolitical implications require sustainable and inclusive policies and measures. Initiatives should focus on supporting the adaptation and resilience of local communities, fostering equitable economic growth, and ensuring the protection of cultural heritage and indigenous rights. Addressing the multifaceted challenges posed by Arctic warming will require global cooperation and commitments to mitigate climate change while ensuring social justice.

- Examination of the economic opportunities brought by shrinking ice in the Arctic

Examination of the Economic Opportunities Brought by Shrinking Ice in the Arctic

THE MELTING OF ICE in the Arctic is undeniably one of the most significant effects of climate change. However, amid concerns about rising sea levels and weather disturbances, there is a silver lining: the economic opportunities presented by the shrinking ice in the Arctic. This article aims to discuss the potential benefits that can be harnessed from this environmental change, shedding light on the implications for commerce, resource extraction, and emerging industries.

Commerce and Shipping:

One of the most apparent opportunities arising from the melting Arctic ice is the opening of new shipping routes. As ice retreats, previously impassable waters become navigable, allowing for shorter transit times between East Asia, Europe, and North America. The Northern Sea Route along Russia's Siberian coast, the Northwest Passage through Canada's Arctic archipelago, and the Transpolar Sea Route are attracting increased attention from global shipping companies.

These alternative routes not only provide an option for reducing costs, fuel consumption, and emissions but also create new commercial opportunities in remote areas previously inaccessible by sea. Improved access to coastal communities, resource-rich regions, and potential tourism destinations not only enhances economic activities but also spurs growth and development in these areas.

Resource Extraction:

The melting Arctic ice also opens up substantial opportunities for resource extraction. The region's vast untapped deposits of oil, natural gas, minerals, and rare earth elements are becoming increasingly accessible. Companies are eagerly eyeing the potential in the Arctic for both traditional and renewable energy resources, creating partnerships and investment opportunities for exploration and exploitation.

The extraction of these resources will not only benefit the economies of Arctic nations; it will also stimulate global economic growth and diversify energy sources. However, the exploitation must be conducted responsibly to mitigate potential environmental risks and threats to fragile ecosystems.

Emerging Industries:

Beyond shipping routes and resource extraction, the melting Arctic ice contributes to the emergence of new industries. The growth of tourism, fishing, and aquaculture provides opportunities for local communities. Unique ecosystems, scenic landscapes, and Arctic wildlife draw in adventure-seeking tourists, stimulating local economies through accommodation, transportation, and associated services.

Furthermore, melting ice facilitates the expansion of fish stocks and the development of aquaculture ventures. Arctic waters could sustain increased fishing activities, providing an economic boost to traditional coastal livelihoods. The prospect of extending aquaculture operations to the region presents enormous potential for food production and opens up yet another revenue stream.

<hr>

WHILE CONCERNS REGARDING climate change remain paramount, it is coherent to consider the associated economic advantages that arise from the shrinking ice in the Arctic. The opening of shipping routes, resource extraction opportunities, and emerging industries all bring with them significant economic potential. However, it is crucial to strike a delicate balance between economic growth and environmental stewardship to ensure sustainable development in the sensitive Arctic ecosystem. Conservation efforts and responsible resource management should be prioritized to protect this delicate region, guaranteeing its long-term prosperity and viability for generations to come.

- Highlighting the implications for oil, gas, and mineral industries

The oil, gas, and mineral industries have long been key players in the global economy. These industries have not only fueled economic growth and development but also played a significant role in shaping geopolitical dynamics. As such, understanding their implications is of utmost importance.

Implications for the oil industry:

1. Environmental concerns: The combustion of oil releases greenhouse gases, contributing to global warming and climate change. As public awareness grows and governments impose stricter regulations, the oil industry is under pressure to transition towards cleaner and more sustainable energy sources.

2. Price volatility: The oil market is notoriously volatile, with prices being influenced by geopolitical tensions, global supply and demand, and market speculation. Fluctuations in oil prices have far-reaching consequences on global economies and can impact the profitability and viability of oil companies.

3. Geopolitical power struggles: Oil-rich countries hold significant leverage and political power in global affairs. Conflicts often arise over access to and control of oil resources, which can lead to tensions and potential military interventions. The geopolitics surrounding oil have shaped historical events and continue to influence international relations.

Implications for the gas industry:

1. Transition to cleaner energy: Natural gas is considered a cleaner alternative to coal and oil, emitting fewer greenhouse gas emissions when burned. As nations strive to reduce their carbon footprint and meet climate change goals, the demand for natural gas is expected to rise, providing growth opportunities for the gas industry.

2. Infrastructure development: Natural gas requires extensive infrastructure for extraction, processing, storage, and distribution. The gas industry plays a vital role in building and maintaining infrastructure, which can create employment opportunities and stimulate economic growth. However,

infrastructure development also raises environmental concerns and may disrupt local communities and ecosystems.

3. Energy security and diversification: Countries seek to reduce their dependence on a single energy source for national security reasons. Gas can offer a diversified energy mix, ensuring greater energy security for nations heavily reliant on oil or coal. The gas industry's influence on shaping energy policies and fostering regional cooperation is crucial for ensuring stability.

Implications for the mineral industry:

1. Resource depletion and competition: The demand for minerals continues to escalate due to industrialization, technological advancements, and population growth. As accessible and high-quality deposits become scarce, mining companies are forced to explore deeper, more challenging terrains, leading to increased exploration costs and environmental risks.

2. Sustaining economic growth: The mineral industry provides the raw materials necessary for various sectors, including construction, electronics, and transportation. A decline in mineral output and scarcity of essential minerals could hinder economic growth and disrupt global supply chains, particularly in developing countries heavily reliant on mineral extraction.

3. Responsible resource management: Mining can have profound ecological and socio-economic impacts, such as habitat destruction, water pollution, and displacement of indigenous communities. As global awareness of these issues grows, mining companies are under increasing pressure to adopt responsible and sustainable practices to minimize negative repercussions and promote community development.

In conclusion, the implications for the oil, gas, and mineral industries are wide-ranging and multi-faceted. These industries contribute significantly to economic growth but also face challenges related to environmental concerns, geopolitics, resource depletion, and sustainable practices. Successfully navigating these implications is crucial for the long-term viability and sustainability of these industries and the global economy as a whole.

- Exploration of the social and cultural impacts of warming on indigenous communities

Exploration of the Social and Cultural Impacts of Warming on Indigenous Communities

THE CONSEQUENCES OF global warming and climate change are felt worldwide, but one particular group severely impacted by these changes is indigenous communities. These communities, who have thrived for centuries in harmony with nature, now face tremendous challenges as their traditional way of life is disrupted by rising temperatures and unpredictable weather patterns. This essay aims to delve into the social and cultural impacts of global warming on indigenous communities, highlighting the profound changes they are facing and the resilience they exhibit in adapting to these challenges.

1. Disruption of Subsistence activities:

Indigenous communities heavily rely on subsistence activities such as hunting, fishing, and farming. Climate change brings about shifts in animal migration patterns, the declining fish population, and altering growing seasons, severely affecting their food sources. This disruption not only undermines traditional sources of sustenance but also their cultural practices and spiritual beliefs; further eroding their connection with the environment and indigenous identity.

2. Loss of Traditional Knowledge:

Indigenous communities possess a unique ecological knowledge passed down from generation to generation. This knowledge, acquired through close observation of their environments, is now at risk due to changing climatic conditions. With the loss of this invaluable traditional knowledge, indigenous communities lose the ability to predict weather patterns, adapt to changes around them, and make informed decisions vital for their survival and preservation of their cultural heritage.

3. Forced Relocation and Resettlement:

Rising sea levels, extreme weather events, and droughts pose threats to entire indigenous communities, compelling them to leave their ancestral lands and relocate. Forced resettlement disrupts important social structures and cultural ties that have been maintained for centuries. These changes often lead to the loss of land rights, cultural traditions, and connection with their spiritual beliefs. Moreover, community cohesion is often undermined when resettlement results in the merging of different tribes, diminishing their unique cultural identities.

4. Mental Health Challenges:

Indigenous communities facing the impacts of climate change endure significant psychological distress. The destruction of their environment, loss of traditional practices, and forced displacement can contribute to feelings of grief, anxiety, and a sense of disconnection from their identity and the natural world they deeply cherish. Mental well-being becomes a crucial focus to support and safeguard community cohesion and cultural resilience in the face of ongoing climatic changes.

<hr>

THE SOCIAL AND CULTURAL impacts of global warming on indigenous communities remain an urgent concern that necessitates immediate attention and action. It is imperative that policymakers, researchers, and the global community work collaboratively to address the challenges faced by these communities. By supporting the rights of indigenous peoples, providing resources to adapt to changing environmental conditions, and promoting sustainable practices, we can help mitigate the negative effects of climate change and ensure the preservation of their unique cultural heritage for future generations.

- Analysis of potential conflicts arising over resource exploitation and sovereignty issues

Analysis of Potential Conflicts Arising over Resource Exploitation and Sovereignty Issues

RESOURCE EXPLOITATION and sovereignty issues have played a significant role in shaping the geopolitical landscape of countries across the globe. As nations strive to meet the demands of growing populations and economies, conflicts related to resource exploitation and the preservation of sovereignty are likely to intensify. This analysis aims to assess the potential conflicts that may arise as a result of resource exploitation and sovereignty issues, highlighting the complex web of political, economic, and environmental factors involved.

1. Competing Interests and Political Rivalries:

One of the primary drivers of conflict in resource exploitation and sovereignty is the presence of competing interests among nations. Countries often have conflicting claims over areas or resources, such as disputed territorial waters or valuable minerals. When economic significance or strategic importance is associated with such resources, political rivalries can escalate into potential conflicts over rights, access, and control.

2. Environmental Concerns:

Resource exploitation is closely intertwined with environmental degradation, leading to potential conflicts between exploitation-driven economic growth and conservation efforts. In regions rich in natural resources, significant tensions may arise between local populations, governments, and environmental activists regarding the environmental impacts of extraction activities, such as oil drilling or mining. Such conflicts can lead to clashes over land rights, pollution control, and sustainable development approaches.

3. Disparities in Economic Benefits:

Resource-rich areas often suffer from a lack of equitable distribution of economic benefits. Key stakeholders, such as multinational corporations or powerful industrialized nations, may exploit resources without adequately compensating local communities or governments. This inherent inequality in resource extraction and its economic benefits can trigger conflicts and political instability, as marginalized groups express dissatisfaction and assert their rights to economic participation.

4. Violations of Sovereignty:

Resource exploitation can raise sovereignty concerns, particularly when foreign companies or nations trespass on the territorial rights of others. Disputes over territorial waters, exclusive economic zones, or offshore resources can escalate tensions and give rise to conflicts, maritime standoffs, or even military confrontations. Asserting sovereignty through territorial defense measures can further destabilize already tense relations, making the situation ripe for potential conflicts.

5. International Cooperation and Diplomacy:

While conflicts may be expected, international cooperation and diplomatic mechanisms can play a pivotal role in de-escalating tensions. Treaties, agreements, and international organizations provide frameworks and forums for nations to address resource-related conflicts peacefully. Dispute resolutions, negotiation processes, and sustainable development initiatives underpinned by diplomatic efforts can alleviate conflicts and promote joint resource management.

<hr>

RESOURCE EXPLOITATION and sovereignty issues remain vital sources of potential conflicts in today's interconnected world. Competing interests, unsustainable practices, environmental concerns, economic disparities, and territorial disputes contribute to the complexities surrounding these conflicts. Nevertheless, international cooperation, diplomacy, and sustainable resource management should be fostered to reduce tensions and ensure that resource exploitation contributes to economic development while respecting sovereignty and environmental sustainability.

Chapter 9: International Collaboration and Policy Responses

In today's interconnected world, collaboration between countries is becoming increasingly important to address common challenges and devise effective solutions. This is especially true when it comes to global issues such as climate change, trade disputes, and public health emergencies. In this chapter, we will explore the importance of international collaboration and examine the various policy responses that are implemented to address these challenges.

International collaboration plays a crucial role in solving complex global problems. No single country can address global challenges alone, as the interconnectedness of our societies and economies requires a collective effort. Through collaboration, countries can share knowledge, resources, and expertise to develop comprehensive solutions that benefit all parties involved.

One area where international collaboration has been paramount is climate change. The effects of climate change are felt globally, and no country is immune to its impacts. The international community has recognized the urgency of this issue and has come together to set targets and implement policies to reduce greenhouse gas emissions. The Paris Agreement, signed by almost all countries in the world, is a prime example of international collaboration on climate change. It sets a global goal to limit global warming to well below 2 degrees Celsius and urges countries to work together to achieve this target.

Trade disputes also require international collaboration to find mutually beneficial solutions. In an interconnected global economy, countries often engage in trade agreements and negotiations to foster economic growth and enhance their competitiveness. However, conflicts and disputes can arise, undermining the benefits of international trade. Collaborative efforts such as multilateral trade agreements and dispute settlement mechanisms aim to resolve these issues fairly and protect the interests of all parties involved.

Public health emergencies, such as pandemics, require rapid response and international cooperation to effectively contain and mitigate their impact. Diseases do not recognize national borders, and a global response is crucial to control outbreaks and prevent the spread of infectious diseases. International organizations such as the World Health Organization (WHO) coordinate efforts between countries, share information and resources, and develop guidelines and best practices to manage public health emergencies. The COVID-19 pandemic has highlighted the importance of international collaboration in responding to such crises, with countries working together to develop vaccines, share medical supplies, and coordinate travel restrictions.

Policy responses to international challenges vary depending on the specific issue at hand. Governments often develop and adopt policy frameworks that reflect the goals and priorities of their country while taking into consideration the global context. These policies can range from domestic regulations to international agreements and treaties.

For climate change, policy responses include setting emission reduction targets, implementing renewable energy incentives, and promoting sustainable practices. Governments may also invest in research and development for clean technologies and support international climate finance initiatives to help developing countries transition to sustainable economies.

In the case of trade disputes, policy responses involve engaging in negotiations, pursuing dispute resolution mechanisms within international organizations such as the World Trade Organization (WTO), and imposing trade tariffs and restrictions when necessary. Countries also strive to enhance market access and create favorable conditions for trade through bilateral and regional agreements.

In the realm of public health, policy responses encompass developing national healthcare systems, ensuring access to essential medicines and vaccines, and investing in disease surveillance and preparedness. Governments also collaborate with international organizations to strengthen global health governance and response mechanisms.

In conclusion, international collaboration is essential for addressing global challenges and developing effective policy responses. Whether it is dealing with climate change, trade disputes, or public health emergencies, no single country can solve these issues alone. By working together, countries can share resources, knowledge, and expertise to devise comprehensive solutions and ensure a better future for all.

- Overview of international efforts to tackle Arctic climate change

Over the past few decades, the Arctic region has been subjected to unprecedented changes due to climate change. Rising temperatures, shrinking sea ice, and changing ecosystems have alerted the international community to the urgent need for tackling Arctic climate change. As a result, numerous international efforts have been initiated to address these challenges and prevent further detrimental consequences.

One significant initiative is the Arctic Climate Impact Assessment (ACIA), conducted by the Arctic Council in collaboration with the International Arctic Science Committee. Released in 2004, the ACIA provided a comprehensive assessment of the current and potential future impacts of climate change in the Arctic. It not only raised awareness but also fueled global discussions on the matter.

The Arctic Council, a high-level intergovernmental forum consisting of Arctic states and six indigenous organizations, has been at the forefront of international efforts. Established in 1996, its objective is to promote cooperation and coordinate actions among member countries on various Arctic issues, including climate change. The council has actively encouraged scientific research, the sharing of data, and the development of policy recommendations to combat Arctic climate change.

The United Nations Framework Convention on Climate Change (UNFCCC) also plays a crucial role in addressing Arctic climate change. The Arctic is considered a particularly vulnerable region, and it is featured prominently in international climate negotiations. The Paris Agreement, adopted in 2015, aims to limit global warming below 2 degrees Celsius and includes provisions to support vulnerable regions like the Arctic. Furthermore, the Intergovernmental Panel on Climate Change (IPCC) regularly assesses the impacts of climate change on the Arctic and contributes to global climate science.

Beyond these international forums, countries have developed bilateral agreements and partnerships to tackle Arctic climate change. For instance, Norway and Russia established the Joint Norwegian-Russian Commission on Environmental Cooperation. This commission focuses on issues like preventing pollution, managing the impact of industrial activities, and improving the conservation of natural resources in the Arctic. Similarly, the United States and Canada have implemented cooperative efforts through the Arctic Council to better understand and mitigate the effects of climate change.

In addition to government-led initiatives, many non-governmental organizations (NGOs) and research institutions are actively engaged in efforts to combat Arctic climate change. These organizations often focus on scientific research, monitoring the impacts of climate change, and proposing policy recommendations. Their work contributes greatly to the global understanding of Arctic climate dynamics and the development of effective measures to protect the region.

While international efforts to tackle Arctic climate change are considerable, challenges persist. One of the main obstacles is the complex governance structure of the Arctic, with multiple stakeholders and competing interests. This often slows decision-making processes and hampers the implementation of cohesive actions. Moreover, funding and resource allocation for Arctic research and mitigation measures remain insufficient to fully address the scale of the challenges.

Overall, the international community recognizes the urgency of addressing Arctic climate change and its broader implications. Global initiatives and partnerships continue to evolve, focusing on scientific research, policy development, and regional cooperation. Through sustained efforts and increased collaboration, it is hoped that international endeavors will lead to effective measures and strategies to mitigate and adapt to the rapidly changing Arctic climate.

- Examination of treaties and agreements aimed at protecting the region

Treaties and agreements play a crucial role in protecting regions from various environmental, social, and economic challenges. These agreements are often comprehensive, incorporating factors such as biodiversity conservation, ecosystem restoration, resource management, and indigenous rights. In this examination, we will delve into some key treaties and agreements that aim to protect specific regions and uncover their significance.

One notable treaty is the Convention on Biological Diversity (CBD), introduced in 1992 at the Earth Summit in Rio de Janeiro. The CBD recognizes the extraordinary value of biological diversity and the urgent need to conserve it. This treaty establishes legally binding obligations for its signatory countries to conserve biological diversity, sustainably use its components, and fairly share the benefits derived from genetic resources. The CBD also emphasizes the involvement of indigenous communities and local stakeholders, acknowledging their invaluable knowledge and practices in conserving biodiversity.

Within the framework of the CBD is the Cartagena Protocol on Biosafety, which addresses concerns associated with the potential risks of modern biotechnology. This protocol focuses on maintaining safety while handling, transferring, and using genetically modified organisms (GMOs). It stipulates that countries should ensure the safe handling, transport, packaging, and labeling of GMOs and establish mechanisms to monitor and manage potential adverse impacts on biodiversity, human health, and socio-economic conditions.

Another well-known agreement is the Ramsar Convention on Wetlands, adopted in Ramsar, Iran, in 1971. The Ramsar Convention aims to halt the worldwide loss of valuable wetland ecosystems and promote their wise use. Wetlands are among the most biologically diverse ecosystems, providing essential habitats for countless species and supporting various ecosystem services. The Ramsar Convention focuses on identifying and protecting wetlands of international importance designated as Ramsar sites and promoting sustainable practices within these areas.

A regional treaty worth examining is the Amazon Cooperation Treaty Organization (ACTO). Formed in 1978, the treaty aims to promote the sustainable development of the Amazon region through regional cooperation and the preservation of the Amazon rainforest. Member countries, including Bolivia, Brazil, Colombia, Ecuador, Guyana, Peru, Suriname, and Venezuela, work together to tackle issues related to deforestation, illegal logging, unsustainable agriculture, and climate change. ACTO helps coordinate joint actions to protect the region's biodiversity and cultural heritage, strengthen sustainable livelihoods, and foster the recognition of indigenous rights in the Amazon basin.

Furthermore, the United Nations Declaration on the Rights of Indigenous Peoples (UNDRIP) is not strictly an environmental treaty but is critical for protecting regions with indigenous populations. Adopted by the UN General Assembly in 2007, UNDRIP recognizes the rights of indigenous peoples to self-determination, cultural identity, lands, resources, and traditional knowledge. It emphasizes the importance of obtaining free, prior, and informed consent from indigenous communities regarding activities that may affect their territories and resources. UNDRIP serves as a framework for ensuring the protection of indigenous rights in treaties and agreements related to regions inhabited by indigenous peoples.

In conclusion, treaties and agreements aimed at protecting regions demonstrate the international community's commitment to environmental conservation, social equity, and sustainable development. Through these instruments, countries come together to address critical issues, establish frameworks for cooperation, and safeguard the unique characteristics of specific regions. Whether it is about biodiversity, wetlands, rainforests, or indigenous rights, these treaties and agreements play a vital role in ensuring the long-term protection and well-being of our planet.

- Analysis of mitigation strategies and adaptation measures

Mitigation strategies and adaptation measures are essential components of climate change action plans. These strategies aim to address the root causes of climate change and to reduce vulnerability and build resilience to its impacts. In this analysis, we will delve into the various mitigation strategies and adaptation measures that are commonly implemented, their effectiveness, and their challenges.

Mitigation strategies primarily focus on reducing greenhouse gas emissions to limit global warming and the resulting climate impacts. These strategies can involve a range of actions, including energy conservation and efficiency, renewable energy deployment, and the reduction of emissions from industries and transportation. Additionally, reforestation and afforestation projects help absorb CO_2 from the atmosphere, further contributing to mitigation efforts.

One of the most impactful mitigation strategies is transitioning from fossil fuels to cleaner energy sources. This involves promoting the use of renewable energy technologies such as solar, wind, and hydro-electric power, which produce little to no greenhouse gas emissions. Governments and businesses around the world have invested heavily in renewable energy infrastructure, resulting in significant emission reductions.

Energy conservation and efficiency measures play a crucial role in mitigating climate change. These measures involve reducing energy waste and optimizing energy use in various sectors. By improving the efficiency of buildings, industrial processes, and transportation systems, substantial emission reductions can be achieved.

The agriculture and forestry sectors also offer significant opportunities for emissions reduction. Sustainable farming practices, such as precision agriculture and organic farming methods, can reduce the use of synthetic fertilizers and decrease methane emissions from livestock. Insensitive and unsustainable practices contribute to deforestation, so implementing more sustainable land management techniques can help sequester atmospheric carbon and minimize emissions from land use change.

While mitigation strategies aim to reduce greenhouse gas emissions, adaptation measures focus on managing the risks and impacts of climate change that cannot be avoided. These measures involve adapting to the changing climate to enhance resilience and reduce vulnerability in different sectors, regions, and communities. Adaptation strategies can include improving infrastructure resilience, enhancing water management systems, and implementing disaster risk reduction measures.

Building resilient infrastructure is a critical adaptation measure. Infrastructure should be designed to withstand extreme weather events and changing climate conditions, reducing the damage caused by storms, flooding, and heatwaves. This can involve upgrading existing infrastructure, improving drainage systems, and utilizing nature-based solutions, such as wetlands, to buffer against floods.

Water management systems also require adaptation to climate change. This includes implementing more efficient irrigation techniques, developing water storage facilities, and improving water allocation methods to cope with increasing water scarcity and shifting rainfall patterns. Additionally, enhancing coastal resilience through the construction of sea walls and restoring natural coastal habitats can protect communities against rising sea levels and storm surges.

Addressing food security is another essential aspect of adaptation to climate change. Changes in temperature and precipitation patterns can significantly impact crop yields and food production. Therefore, promoting climate-resilient agricultural practices, improving farmer access to climate information and early warning systems, and diversifying food sources are critical adaptation measures for ensuring food security.

Implementing effective mitigation strategies and adaptation measures face numerous challenges. One significant challenge is the allocation of financial resources to support these actions. Adequate funding is required to implement large-scale renewable energy projects, develop climate-resilient infrastructure, and support vulnerable communities in adapting to climate change impacts.

Technical and institutional barriers can also hinder the implementation of mitigation and adaptation measures. Limited technological know-how and capacity, as well as bureaucratic hurdles, can slow down the progress of projects. Coordinating efforts among multiple stakeholders, including governments, organizations, and local communities, is crucial for successful implementation.

Furthermore, public awareness and political will play a vital role in fulfilling climate change action plans. Sustaining public support and political commitment is necessary to ensure the long-term implementation and effectiveness of mitigation strategies and adaptation measures.

In conclusion, mitigation strategies and adaptation measures are integral to addressing climate change impacts. By reducing greenhouse gas emissions and building resilience, these actions contribute to a sustainable and climate-resilient future. However, challenges such as financial constraints, technical obstacles, and the need for political will must be addressed to successfully implement and scale-up these actions.

- Evaluation of the effectiveness of current policies and areas for improvement

When it comes to evaluating the effectiveness of current policies, there are several key factors to consider. These include the desired outcomes of the policy, the methods by which those outcomes are measured, and the actual impact that the policy has had on the intended population or area. By thoroughly examining these aspects, policymakers and stakeholders can determine both the successes of current policies and areas in need of improvement.

One of the first steps in evaluating policy effectiveness is clearly defining the desired outcomes. This involves setting specific goals and objectives that the policy is meant to achieve. For example, a policy aimed at reducing greenhouse gas emissions might have the goal of decreasing emissions by a certain percentage within a specific time frame. By clearly articulating these outcomes, it becomes easier to measure and assess the effectiveness of the policy.

Once the desired outcomes have been defined, it is important to establish methods for measuring progress towards those outcomes. This may involve using quantitative data, such as the number of participants benefiting from the policy or changes in key indicators, or qualitative data, such as survey responses and interviews. By collecting and analyzing relevant data, policymakers can better understand the impact the policy is having and identify areas where improvements may be needed.

In assessing the actual impact of a policy, it is crucial to take into account any unintended consequences or negative effects. For example, a policy aimed at reducing income inequality may inadvertently create incentives that discourage individuals from seeking higher-paying jobs. By analyzing and addressing these unintended consequences, policymakers can fine-tune their strategies and make improvements to the policy.

In addition to evaluating the effectiveness of current policies, it is equally important to identify areas for improvement. This involves analyzing the data collected during the evaluation process and identifying any gaps or weaknesses in the current policy approach. For instance, if a policy aimed at improving educational outcomes for disadvantaged students is showing limited success, it may be necessary to explore alternative strategies, such as increased investment in early childhood education or targeted interventions. By acknowledging areas for improvement, policymakers can adapt and refine their policies to maximize their impact.

Furthermore, involving stakeholders and seeking their input can provide valuable insights into the effectiveness of current policies and areas for improvement. This may involve conducting consultations, engaging with communities, or soliciting feedback through surveys and public forums. Such engagement facilitates a bottom-up approach to policy evaluation and can help ensure that the voices and perspectives of those directly affected by the policy are taken into consideration.

In conclusion, an evaluation of the effectiveness of current policies requires a comprehensive examination of desired outcomes, methods of measurement, and impact assessment. It is essential to gather and analyze relevant data, consider unintended consequences, and involve stakeholders throughout the process. By doing so, policymakers can identify areas for improvement and refine their strategies to better address the needs of the population or area in question.

Chapter 10: Future Scenarios and Potential Solutions

In this chapter, we will explore various future scenarios and potential solutions to the challenges we may face in the coming years. With the rapid advancements in technology, climate change concerns, and other global issues, it is essential to consider multiple possibilities and develop strategies accordingly. We will delve into four different future scenarios: business as usual, technocratic paradise, environmental triumph, and societal collapse. Each scenario brings forth unique challenges and potential solutions, providing us with a comprehensive understanding of the paths that lie ahead.

1. Business as Usual:

In this scenario, we envision a future where current systems and practices continue without significant alteration or reform. While this may seem like the most plausible scenario, it comes with its fair share of challenges. Issues like inequality, resource depletion, and economic instability would persist and potentially worsen. One potential solution would be to implement regulations and policies that promote sustainable business practices, reduce inequalities, and mitigate environmental impact. Encouraging companies to adopt circular economies, invest in renewable energy, and prioritize social responsibility could help steer us away from a bleak future.

2. Technocratic Paradise:

In this scenario, the focus is on advanced technology and innovation shaping a paradise-like society. While advancements in science and technology can offer numerous benefits, their potential negative consequences cannot be overlooked. Striking a balance between technological advancements and ethical considerations is crucial here. Implementing frameworks that prioritize transparency, public participation, and long-term safety assessments could help minimize the risk associated with technological overreach. Additionally, policies that prioritize research and development for sustainability and social impact must be embraced to avoid a technocratic dystopia.

3. Environmental Triumph:

This scenario imagines a future where humankind successfully addresses environmental challenges and creates a sustainable and resilient society. To achieve this, it will be essential to implement comprehensive policies that tackle climate change, protect biodiversity, and promote ecological restoration. Embracing renewable energy sources, incentivizing sustainable agriculture practices, and investing in green infrastructure could play key roles in achieving environmental triumph. It also requires international cooperation and collaborative efforts among governments, businesses, and communities to address environmental concerns on a global scale.

4. Societal Collapse:

This scenario presents a future where various socio-political and environmental factors lead to the collapse of societies. While it may sound dire, exploring potential solutions becomes crucial for ensuring our preparedness in addressing these challenges. Building resilient communities and promoting social cohesion through education, empowerment, and local governance could serve as a potential solution. Similarly, adopting sustainable practices that prioritize self-reliance, diversification, and resource conservation could mitigate the risks associated with societal collapse.

⸻ ◉ ⸻

THE FUTURE IS UNCERTAIN, and preparing for multiple scenarios is crucial for our collective well-being. Each scenario discussed here presents unique challenges and compels us to take proactive measures in shaping a desirable path. Aligning our policies, harnessing the power of technology responsibly, embracing sustainability, and fostering collaboration among diverse stakeholders can help us navigate the uncertainties and create a more prosperous and harmonious future. The choices we make today can significantly impact the scenarios we encounter tomorrow.

- Exploration of projected future scenarios for Arctic warming

Arctic warming has become one of the most pressing issues in recent times, attracting global attention due to its potential environmental and socio-economic consequences. As temperatures continue to rise at extraordinary rates, it has become crucial to explore and establish projected future scenarios for Arctic warming in order to fully grasp the gravity of the situation and devise effective mitigation and adaptation strategies.

One of the most noticeable effects of Arctic warming is the melting of glaciers and polar ice caps. This phenomenon has led to an increase in sea levels, posing a threat to low-lying coastal areas and small island nations. The Intergovernmental Panel on Climate Change (IPCC) predicts that by the year 2100, global sea levels could rise by approximately 1 meter, with the Arctic region experiencing even higher increments.

Furthermore, the melting of sea ice exposes darker ocean surfaces, which absorbs more solar radiation compared to the reflective nature of ice. This positive feedback loop contributes to increased warming in the region. Climate models indicate that this trend will continue in the foreseeable future, potentially resulting in a drastic reduction of summer Arctic sea ice by as soon as 2030. The implications of this scenario are far-reaching and include disruptions in wildlife habitats, altered oceanic currents, and changes in regional and global climate patterns.

Projected future scenarios for Arctic warming also indicate potential shifts in ecosystems and the distribution of species. The Arctic region is home to a diverse range of plants and animals that have adapted to the specialized conditions. However, as the climate rapidly changes, these ecosystems face severe disruptions. Species like polar bears, which depend on sea ice for hunting, are particularly vulnerable. Without swift intervention, it is projected that polar bear populations could decline by up to two-thirds by the end of the century.

The melting of permafrost, a layer of permanently frozen soil, is yet another concern in projected future scenarios for Arctic warming. Permafrost contains a significant amount of stored carbon, and as it thaws, that carbon is released into the atmosphere in the form of carbon dioxide and methane- greenhouse gases that further contribute to global warming. Scientists predict that if warming continues at current rates, the release of these gases could accelerate, exacerbating the effects of climate change.

The geopolitical consequences of Arctic warming present additional challenges in envisioning the future scenarios for the region. With the melting of sea ice, new shipping routes become accessible, opening up the possibility for increased maritime trade. This could lead to a shift in global transportation patterns and economic dynamics. However, the abundance of resources, particularly fossil fuels, in the Arctic will likely spark competition among nations, potentially leading to political tensions.

In the face of these projected future scenarios, addressing and mitigating Arctic warming requires a multifaceted approach. International cooperation is imperative to effectively reduce greenhouse gas emissions and limit global warming. Adaptation strategies must also be implemented to safeguard vulnerable ecosystems, plant and animal species, and indigenous communities who depend on the Arctic for their livelihoods.

Research efforts, technological advances, and innovative solutions should be focused on developing sustainable energy sources, reducing carbon emissions, and enhancing climate modeling capabilities. Additionally, scientific collaborations that assess the socio-economic and health impacts of Arctic warming are crucial for informed policy-making and fostering resilience in affected regions.

In conclusion, the exploration of projected future scenarios for Arctic warming presents a vivid picture of the severity and complexity of the challenges ahead. From rising sea levels and the loss of sea ice to ecosystem disruptions and geopolitical implications, the impact of Arctic warming resonates on a global scale. Taking proactive measures, prioritizing sustainability, and fostering international cooperation are key to addressing this pressing issue and ensuring a sustainable future for the Arctic and beyond.

- Analysis of potential solutions to mitigate and adapt to climate change

Climate change is one of the most pressing issues facing our planet today. It's causing rising global temperatures, extreme weather events, rising sea levels, and changing precipitation patterns, among other devastating impacts. To combat these effects, it's crucial to consider and analyze potential solutions to mitigate and adapt to climate change.

Mitigation refers to efforts aimed at reducing greenhouse gas emissions to prevent further climate change. One potential solution is shifting towards renewable sources of energy, such as solar and wind power. These sources have significantly lower carbon footprints compared to fossil fuels, making them a cleaner and more sustainable option. Additionally, phasing out coal-powered plants and replacing them with greener alternatives can greatly reduce carbon emissions.

Energy efficiency is another important aspect of climate change mitigation. Encouraging individuals and industries to adopt energy-efficient practices can reduce energy consumption and therefore decrease greenhouse gas emissions. This can involve simple actions like using energy-efficient appliances, improving insulation, implementing stricter building codes, and promoting public transport.

Another potential solution to mitigate climate change is carbon capture and storage (CCS). This involves capturing CO_2 emissions from power plants and industrial facilities and permanently storing them underground. CCS has the potential to reduce a significant amount of CO_2 emissions, but it requires further research and development to make it economically feasible and environmentally safe.

Adapting to the impacts of climate change is equally important as mitigating it. This can involve implementing measures to protect vulnerable coastal areas from rising sea levels and storm surges. Building sea walls, creating mangrove buffers, and implementing sand nourishments are all potential solutions to protect these regions.

Water management is another crucial aspect of climate change adaptation. As rainfall patterns become less predictable and droughts become more frequent, it's essential to implement efficient water management strategies. This can involve collecting and storing rainwater for future use, implementing better irrigation techniques in agriculture, and managing water resources to ensure their sustainable use.

Furthermore, implementing nature-based solutions can play a significant role in climate change adaptation. Conserving and restoring natural ecosystems like forests, wetlands, and coral reefs can help regulate climate patterns and provide natural buffers against extreme weather events. These habitats act as carbon sinks, meaning they absorb CO2 from the atmosphere, helping mitigate climate change impacts.

Additionally, focusing on climate education and awareness is crucial to drive policy changes and individual actions. Educating the public about the impacts of climate change and empowering individuals to adopt sustainable practices can lead to a broader adoption of solutions.

In conclusion, addressing climate change requires a multi-faceted approach that encompasses both mitigation and adaptation strategies. Shifting towards renewable energy sources, promoting energy efficiency, implementing carbon capture and storage, protecting vulnerable coastal areas, managing water resources efficiently, and implementing nature-based solutions are all potential ways to mitigate and adapt to climate change. However, these solutions would require collaboration, policy changes, investment, and technological advancements to be effective on a global scale. With concerted efforts, we have the potential to mitigate the future impacts of climate change and create a more sustainable future.

- Discussion on the role of renewable energy sources and sustainable practices

Renewable energy sources and sustainable practices play a crucial role in addressing the urgent need for transitioning to a cleaner and more sustainable future. As the world grapples with the challenges posed by climate change, the conversation surrounding these topics has gained significant importance and momentum. This discussion aims to explore the vital role that renewable energy sources and sustainable practices play in mitigating climate change and promoting a more sustainable society.

One of the main reasons renewable energy sources are gaining popularity is their potential to reduce greenhouse gas emissions. Unlike fossil fuels, which emit significant amounts of carbon dioxide, renewable energy sources such as solar, wind, and hydropower produce little to no greenhouse gases during operation. The use of these clean energy sources can significantly contribute to reducing global carbon emissions and combatting climate change.

Moreover, renewable energy sources are virtually infinite and naturally replenished. Unlike finite fossil fuel resources that deplete over time, renewable energy sources offer a sustainable and abundant energy supply. Access to sustainable energy could also foster economic growth, especially in developing regions where traditional forms of energy may be inaccessible. Furthermore, renewable energy can help reduce dependence on fossil fuels, potentially decreasing geopolitical tensions associated with resource scarcity and diminishing the environmental impacts of fossil fuel extraction.

On the other hand, sustainable practices encompass a broad range of behaviors and initiatives aimed at reducing environmental damage and promoting long-term ecological balance. These practices go beyond the energy sector and extend to areas such as agriculture, waste management, transportation, and construction, to name a few.

In agriculture, for instance, sustainable practices promote organic farming, agroforestry, crop rotation, and other methods that minimize soil erosion, prevent chemical pollution, and enhance biodiversity. Similarly, in transportation, the shift toward electric vehicles and the expansion of public transport systems contribute to reducing greenhouse gas emissions and addressing air pollution.

From a waste management perspective, sustainable practices focus on recycling, composting, and adopting circular economy principles to reduce the reliance on landfills and unsustainable waste disposal methods. Sustainable construction, on the other hand, emphasizes the use of eco-friendly materials, energy-efficient designs, and green building techniques to reduce emissions and improve overall resource efficiency.

Implementing sustainable practices requires a multidimensional approach with collective effort from individuals, businesses, and governments. Education and awareness campaigns can raise public consciousness about sustainable living and drive behavior change.

Governments, in particular, play a crucial role in creating an enabling policy environment that incentivizes the adoption of renewable energy sources and sustainable practices. Policies such as feed-in tariffs, tax incentives, and renewable portfolio standards can accelerate the deployment of renewable energy technologies and encourage businesses and individuals to transition to cleaner energy sources.

While the implementation of renewable energy sources and sustainable practices has numerous benefits, there are also challenges that need to be addressed. The intermittency of renewable energy sources like solar and wind can hinder their widespread adoption, necessitating the development of energy storage technologies and smart grid systems. Additionally, the upfront costs of renewable energy systems can still be a barrier to entry for some communities and countries, requiring further investment and financial support mechanisms.

In conclusion, the role of renewable energy sources and sustainable practices in addressing climate change and promoting a sustainable future cannot be understated. From reducing greenhouse gas emissions and protecting biodiversity to promoting economic development and resource efficiency, these initiatives offer a holistic approach to the urgent environmental challenges we face. By leveraging the potential of renewable energy sources, implementing sustainable practices, and fostering collaboration at various levels, we can pave the way for a cleaner, healthier, and more sustainable world.

- Examination of proposed geoengineering techniques and their ethical considerations

Examination of Proposed Geoengineering Techniques and Their Ethical Considerations

GEOENGINEERING REFERS to deliberate adjustments to the Earth's climate system in order to counteract or mitigate the impacts of climate change. As the urgency to address climate change intensifies, a range of proposed geoengineering techniques have emerged. These techniques aim to artificially manipulate different aspects of our environment, challenging ethical dilemmas that society should carefully consider. This article delves into the various emerging geoengineering techniques while critically examining their ethical implications.

1. Solar Radiation Management (SRM):

SRM techniques involve reducing the amount of sunlight that reaches the Earth's surface, thereby blocking and reflecting a portion of solar radiation. These techniques include stratospheric aerosol injection, where reflective particles are injected into the stratosphere. While SRM shows potential in reducing global temperatures, it raises concerns regarding unintended consequences, fairness, and international governance. The risks associated with regional climate impacts and dependency on continuous implementation must also be scrutinized ethically.

2. Afforestation and Carbon Capture:

Afforestation involves the large-scale planting of trees to capture and store carbon dioxide. Carbon Capture and Storage (CCS) technologies, on the other hand, aim to capture carbon emissions from power plants and store them underground. These techniques offer certain environmental benefits but raise ethical concerns relating to land-use, land rights, and resource management, particularly in developing countries. Ensuring equitable distribution of impacts and fostering inclusivity during project planning are crucial challenges.

3. Ocean Iron Fertilization:

This technique involves adding iron to the ocean to stimulate plankton growth, which in turn absorbs carbon dioxide through photosynthesis. While seemingly beneficial for reducing atmospheric carbon levels, ocean iron fertilization carries ethical dilemmas relating to ecosystem disruption, unknown consequences on marine life, and potential interference with local economies or traditional practices. Environmental precaution, consent from local communities, and robust regulatory frameworks are imperative in assessing this technique ethically.

4. Weather Modification:

Weather modification techniques involve altering cloud properties or modifying precipitation patterns to address regional water scarcity challenges. Cloud seeding is one such technique that disperses substances into clouds to encourage rain formation. The ethical considerations surrounding weather modification revolve around issues of control, unintended impacts on ecological systems, regulatory oversight, and ensuring transparency during implementation.

5. Direct Air Capture (DAC) and Enhanced Weathering:

DAC technologies aim to capture carbon dioxide directly from the atmosphere for storage or utilization. Enhanced weathering, sometimes referred to as carbon mineralization, involves accelerating natural weathering processes to store carbon dioxide in minerals like olivine or limestone. Ethical concerns with these techniques include their energy and resource requirements, potential inequitable access to technology, the long-term stability of carbon storage, and potential disturbances to local ecosystems.

⎯⎯⎯◉⎯⎯⎯

GEOENGINEERING TECHNIQUES hold promise in potentially mitigating the effects of climate change; however, thorough examination of their ethical considerations is vital. The intertwined nature of environmental, societal, and technological aspects necessitates robust debate and ethical frameworks to guide their development and implementation responsibly. By rigorously evaluating potential risks and benefits, fostering transparency, and incorporating the perspectives and rights of affected communities, we can pave the way for ethically feasible and sustainable geoengineering solutions.

Chapter 11: Understanding the Arctic's Importance in the Global Climate System

The Arctic region has always fascinated scientists and explorers with its extreme landscapes, unique wildlife, and rich natural resources. However, in recent years, it has gained even more attention due to its crucial role in the global climate system. The purpose of this chapter is to delve into the detailed and fascinating information surrounding the Arctic's importance in the global climate system. By understanding the factors at play here, we can gain valuable insights into the potential impacts of climate change and devise effective strategies to mitigate its consequences.

1. The Arctic Amplification Phenomenon:

One of the key features of the Arctic region is its vulnerability to climate change, resulting in a phenomenon known as Arctic amplification. Due to various feedback mechanisms, such as the ice-albedo feedback, the Arctic is warming at a rate more than twice as fast as the global average. This amplified warming not only leads to the accelerated melting of Arctic sea ice but also affects the regional weather patterns and can even influence the global climate system.

2. Albedo and the Melting Arctic Sea Ice:

The Arctic sea ice, which covers vast expanses of the Arctic Ocean, plays a crucial role in maintaining the region's climate balance. Its bright surface reflects a significant portion of the incoming solar radiation back into space, thereby keeping the region relatively cool. However, as the sea ice melts due to global warming, a darker surface is exposed, reducing the albedo and thus absorbing more solar radiation. This amplifies the warming process and leads to further ice melt, creating a positive feedback loop with significant implications.

3. Impacts on the Arctic Ecosystem:

The melting of Arctic sea ice disrupts the delicate balance of the region's ecosystem. Polar bears, which rely on sea ice as platforms for hunting seals, are facing food shortages and reduced breeding success. Additionally, other species, including Arctic foxes, walruses, and certain bird populations, are also experiencing significant disruptions. Changes in sea ice cover and melting permafrost can also disturb marine productivity, affecting aquatic life and the entire food chain within the Arctic region.

4. Arctic and the Global Climate:

While the impact of climate change in the Arctic is first and most directly felt in this region, it also has far-reaching consequences for the rest of the planet. The warming Arctic disrupts atmospheric circulation patterns, influencing global weather patterns, and potentially leading to extreme weather events such as heatwaves, flooding, and more. The melting Arctic glaciers also contribute to rising sea levels globally, threatening coastal communities around the world.

5. The Role of Arctic Feedback Loops:

Feedback loops in the Arctic region add complexity to the already intricate global climate system. For example, as melting permafrost releases methane, a potent greenhouse gas, it contributes to further warming. This additional warming then accelerates permafrost thaw, leading to more methane emissions, forming a concerning feedback loop. Understanding and accurately modeling these feedback loops are crucial for predicting future climate scenarios and devising effective strategies to mitigate climate change.

<hr>

IN CONCLUSION, THE Arctic plays a pivotal role in the global climate system due to a combination of factors such as the Arctic amplification phenomenon, albedo changes, impacts on ecosystems, and feedback loops. The rapid changes occurring in the Arctic have far-reaching consequences for the whole planet, including sea-level rise, weather pattern disruptions, and threats to biodiversity. By studying and understanding these intricacies, we can take necessary actions to limit the impacts of climate change and preserve the Arctic's importance in our global climate system for future generations.

- Overview of the Arctic's role in regulating global climate

The Arctic region plays a crucial role in regulating global climate. It is not only a unique and beautiful part of our planet, but also a vital component of the Earth's climate system. This overview delves into the various ways in which the Arctic impacts global climate and why it is essential to understand and protect this fragile environment.

One of the primary ways in which the Arctic regulates global climate is through its role as a reflector of solar radiation. The icy landscapes of the region, such as the sea ice and snow cover, have high albedo. Albedo refers to the ability of a surface to reflect sunlight. The bright white ice and snow in the Arctic reflect a significant portion of the incoming solar radiation back into space, preventing it from being absorbed by the Earth's surface.

This reflection of solar radiation helps to cool down the Arctic and plays a critical role in maintaining the planet's temperature balance. If the Arctic ice were to melt, exposing darker surfaces like the ocean, these surfaces would absorb more sunlight, leading to further warming and accelerated melting. This positive feedback mechanism, known as the ice-albedo feedback, could have far-reaching consequences for global climate by amplifying the pace of global warming.

Another crucial aspect of the Arctic's role in regulating global climate is its influence on atmospheric circulation patterns. The Arctic acts as a control tower for atmospheric circulation, influencing weather patterns and climate systems around the world. Due to the region's high latitude, there is a stark contrast in temperature between the cold Arctic and the warmer equator. This temperature difference drives the circulation of air masses, impacting wind patterns and transnational weather systems.

However, with the intensification of climate change, the Arctic is experiencing a rapid decrease in sea ice extent. This loss of sea ice has disrupted the atmospheric circulation patterns, resulting in more frequent extreme weather events in some parts of the world. Researchers have observed changes in the jet stream, which can cause persistent weather patterns and extreme temperature deviations, such as prolonged heatwaves or cold snaps.

The melting of the Arctic ice also contributes to rising sea levels. Melting sea ice does not directly raise sea levels since it already displaces its mass in the water. However, the melting of land-locked ice masses like glaciers stored in Greenland contributes to sea level rise. As the Arctic warms, the melting of the Greenland ice sheet increases, adding freshwater to the oceans and contributing to the global increase in sea levels.

Furthermore, the Arctic region plays a crucial role in the carbon cycle and the global carbon budget. The soils, vegetation, and permafrost found in the Arctic store vast amounts of organic carbon. Permafrost, which is permanently frozen ground, holds great quantities of carbon in the form of frozen vegetation and ancient organic material. However, rising temperatures are causing permafrost to thaw, leading to the release of carbon dioxide and methane gases into the atmosphere. Methane is a potent greenhouse gas, contributing to further warming and exacerbating the effects of climate change.

This overview highlights the complexity of the Arctic's role in regulating global climate. Its reflective properties, atmospheric influences, impact on sea levels, and contribution to the global carbon cycle are all interconnected. As climate warming contributes to the ongoing thawing of the Arctic, it triggers a range of feedback mechanisms that may intensify global warming and have far-reaching consequences for the Earth's climate system.

Understanding and protecting the Arctic environment are crucial for mitigating the effects of climate change. Conservation efforts, advocating for sustainable practices, and reducing greenhouse gas emissions can contribute to preserving the Arctic and maintaining its vital role in regulating global climate. Proper management of the Arctic is not only crucial for the continued survival of its unique ecosystems but also for the well-being and sustainability of our entire planet.

- Examination of feedback loops and system complexities

In the field of systems thinking and analysis, feedback loops play a critical role in understanding the complexities of a system. Feedback loops are self-regulating mechanisms that help maintain a balance and stability within a system. They can either be reinforcing or balancing.

Reinforcing feedback loops occur when an initial change in a system leads to further changes that reinforce the original change. This can result in a loop of continuous growth or decline. For example, the increase in greenhouse gases leads to global warming, which in turn increases the release of even more greenhouse gases, exacerbating the warming effect.

Balancing feedback loops, on the other hand, work to stabilize the system by counteracting any changes that deviate from the desired state. These loops are characterized by feedback mechanisms that tend to oppose the initial change, bringing the system back to equilibrium. An example of a balancing feedback loop can be seen in the regulation of body temperature. When the body becomes too hot, sweating is triggered, which helps in cooling down the body and bringing its temperature back to a normal range.

Understanding these feedback loops is fundamental for analyzing complex systems since they often give rise to unexpected behaviors and phenomena. When multiple feedback loops interact with each other, they can amplify, dampen, or moderate the overall system behavior, giving rise to complex and often non-linear dynamics.

In complex systems, the relationship between the system's components and their interactions can result in emergent properties, which are properties that do not exist at the individual component level but arise from the interactions between those components.

For instance, consider a traffic network. Each vehicle's movement is influenced by the movements of other vehicles on the road. When there is congestion, it can create a domino effect, causing delays and even gridlock in certain areas. This emergent behavior arises from interactions between individual drivers, their decisions, and the feedback loops created by their collective behavior.

Examining feedback loops and system complexities is crucial for understanding and predicting the behavior of systems. It helps identify the underlying causes of problems and reveals opportunities for intervention and improvement.

Moreover, in complex systems, it is necessary to consider various interconnected components and feedback loops that can interact and affect each other. These interactions can be indirect and delayed, which makes it even more challenging to predict the system's behavior accurately.

The role of technology in analyzing feedback loops and system complexities has been growing significantly. Advanced computer simulations and modeling techniques allow researchers to simulate and experiment with different scenarios, making it easier to understand the dynamics and behaviors of complex systems.

Practitioners in various fields, such as environmental science, engineering, and business management, as well as policymakers, are increasingly using systems thinking tools to better comprehend complex systems' behavior and develop effective strategies for managing them.

In conclusion, examining feedback loops and system complexities is essential for understanding how systems function and behave. Whether it is in natural or man-made systems, feedback loops play a crucial role in governing their dynamics. The intertwined nature of feedback loops and emergent properties makes it necessary to analyze and consider multiple components and their interactions to gain insights into system behavior.

- Discussion on the implications for global climate change mitigation efforts

Global climate change mitigation efforts have far-reaching implications for the future of our planet. The need to address this urgent issue has become increasingly evident as the impacts of climate change continue to intensify around the world. In order to effectively reduce greenhouse gas emissions and limit global warming, countries from all corners of the globe have been working diligently to implement mitigation strategies. These efforts span across sectors, ranging from energy production and transportation to land use and agriculture.

One of the key implications of global climate change mitigation efforts is the transition to renewable and cleaner forms of energy. Fossil fuels are major contributors to greenhouse gas emissions, and reducing their consumption is crucial in order to achieve the emissions targets set in the Paris Agreement. Many countries have started investing heavily in renewable energy technologies such as solar, wind, and hydropower. These efforts not only promote cleaner energy sources but also support technological advancements and job creation in the renewable energy sector.

Another important implication for global climate change mitigation efforts is the need to address deforestation and unsustainable land use practices. Forests act as carbon sinks, absorbing large amounts of CO_2 from the atmosphere. However, deforestation and land degradation result in the release of carbon stored in trees and soils, further exacerbating climate change. To combat this issue, countries are implementing policies and programs aimed at reducing deforestation, promoting reforestation, and sustainable land management practices.

Furthermore, global climate change mitigation efforts require enhanced international cooperation and policy coordination. Climate change is a global issue that transcends national boundaries, making it essential for countries to work together towards a common goal. The Paris Agreement serves as a testament to this international collaboration, as it brings countries together in their commitment to reduce greenhouse gas emissions and limit global temperature rise. Through regular meetings and negotiations, countries are able to share knowledge and best practices, encouraging the development of collective solutions.

In addition, an important implication for global climate change mitigation efforts is the consideration of equity and social justice. The impacts of climate change are not evenly distributed, with vulnerable communities and countries often hit the hardest. Mitigation actions should ensure that they are not exacerbating social disparity and instead prioritize the needs and interests of those most affected. This means helping developing nations transition to low-carbon economies and providing financial and technological support to countries that are less equipped to deal with the challenges of climate change.

Ultimately, the success of global climate change mitigation efforts relies on a combination of factors. It requires strong political will, effective policies and regulations, technological innovation, and significant investment. Furthermore, efforts to mitigate climate change must be systemic and holistic, addressing not only the reduction of emissions but also adapting to the impacts that are already occurring. By considering and addressing these implications, we can work towards a sustainable and resilient future for our planet.

- Analysis of the interconnectedness between the Arctic and other regions

The interconnectedness between the Arctic and other regions is a complex web of relationships that spans economic, political, social, and environmental dimensions. This analysis will explore the various ways in which the Arctic influences and is influenced by other regions, shedding light on the importance of this remote and often overlooked corner of the globe.

Economically, the Arctic region plays a crucial role in global trade and resource extraction. The melting sea ice has opened up new shipping routes through the Arctic Ocean, reducing travel distances and costs for international trade between Europe and Asia. This has important implications for the economies of countries like Russia, Canada, and Norway, which have invested heavily in developing ports and infrastructure along these newly accessible routes. International shipping companies also benefit from the shorter travel times and the potential for reduced energy consumption that the Arctic routes offer.

Furthermore, the Arctic is rich in natural resources, including oil, gas, minerals, and fish stocks. The extraction of these resources is a significant driver of economic activity in the region and a source of large-scale investment. Many countries, particularly those with territory within the Arctic Circle, have staked claims and engaged in disputes over resource rights, indicating the strategic importance of the region in terms of energy security and access to mineral reserves.

Beyond its economic significance, the Arctic is intricately linked to other regions through environmental and climatic factors. Climate change, resulting from global greenhouse gas emissions, is drastically altering the Arctic landscape. The rapid melting of ice, rising sea levels, and changing weather patterns have far-reaching consequences for ecosystems and communities beyond the region. The reduced albedo effect caused by decreasing ice coverage in the Arctic leads to increased absorption of sunlight, exacerbating global warming. This interconnectedness has increasingly put the Arctic at the center of global discussions on climate change and has spurred collaborative efforts among nations to mitigate its effects.

Politically, the Arctic is a region of great interest and rivalry. As the likelihood of resource extraction and increased commercial activities grows, so does geopolitical competition. The eight nations that have territory within the Arctic Circle – Russia, Canada, the United States, Denmark (Greenland and the Faroe Islands), Sweden, Finland, Norway, and Iceland – have competing claims and overlapping interests in the region. In recent years, there has been an uptick in military posturing and a renewed focus on defense capabilities in the Arctic, fueling concerns of potential conflicts in the future. International cooperation and diplomatic efforts are often needed to resolve disputes and prevent escalations.

Lastly, the Arctic and its unique indigenous communities are directly influenced by social factors and policies in other regions. Indigenous peoples, such as the Inuit, Saami, and indigenous Siberians, have long-standing connections to the Arctic and rely on its resources for their livelihoods and cultural practices. Changes in the Arctic ecosystem not only impact their traditional ways of life but also affect wider issues of indigenous rights and self-determination. As regional and national policies on Indigenous rights and conservation evolve, the Arctic communities are increasingly interconnected with global networks advocating for recognition and protection.

In conclusion, the interconnectedness between the Arctic and other regions is multifaceted and far-reaching. From economic and environmental impacts to political rivalries and social implications, the Arctic plays a crucial role in shaping global dynamics. As global interest in the region continues to grow, the need for sustainable management, collaborative governance, and equitable policies becomes increasingly apparent. Recognizing the interconnectedness between the Arctic and other regions is essential for maintaining the delicate balance between human activities and the long-term health of this vulnerable and remarkable ecosystem.

Chapter 12: Inequality and Environmental Justice in the Arctic

In recent decades, discussions surrounding environmental justice and inequality have gained significant traction across various regions of the world. The Arctic, with its unique characteristics and increasingly visible changes due to climate change, presents a gripping case study to examine these socio-environmental issues. This chapter delves into the intricate relationship between inequality and environmental justice in the Arctic, providing a comprehensive analysis of the factors driving these phenomena and their implications for both human societies and the natural environment.

Understanding Inequality in the Arctic:

To comprehend the complexity of inequality in the Arctic, it is crucial to consider historical and contemporary factors that have shaped this disparity. Throughout history, the Arctic has been inhabited by indigenous populations who have often faced marginalization and unequal power dynamics within larger nation-states. The legacies of colonization and economic exploitation have further exacerbated socio-economic disparities, leading to a persistent inequality in the region. Inequality manifests itself in various forms, including differences in access to resources, representation, and decision-making power.

Environmental Injustice in the Arctic:

Environmental justice refers to the fair and equitable distribution of environmental benefits and burdens. Despite having contributed minimally to global greenhouse gas emissions and climate change, Arctic indigenous communities bear the brunt of the environmental burdens resulting from such shifts. Melting ice caps, rising sea levels, and changes in local ecosystems not only pose immediate threats to their traditional ways of life but also have long-term implications for their socio-cultural integrity. Moreover, the phenomenon of "environmental colonialism" arises as multinational corporations exploit the region's natural resources without adequately involving or considering the needs of Arctic communities.

Climate Change and Amplified Inequality:

The rapid rate at which climate change affects the Arctic magnifies inequality in the region. Arctic communities, particularly indigenous peoples, are often more vulnerable due to a variety of factors such as limited access to resources, infrastructure, and healthcare systems. Disruptions caused by changing weather patterns, depletion of wildlife, and glacial melting strongly impact indigenous livelihoods, exacerbating existing inequality. This disproportionate vulnerability further reinforces the need for environmental justice in the Arctic.

Political and Economic Challenges:

Political and economic factors play a significant role in perpetuating inequality in the Arctic. Geopolitical interests, driven by the race for untapped natural resources, have intensified the risk of marginalization for indigenous communities. The select few with access to political and economic power dictate resource extraction policies that rarely prioritize the needs and welfare of the region's inhabitants. Consequently, environmental justice becomes increasingly elusive as short-term economic gains take precedence over long-term socio-environmental sustainability.

Pathways to Environmental Justice:

Addressing inequality and achieving environmental justice in the Arctic requires a multi-faceted approach. First and foremost, empowering indigenous communities to take an active role in decision-making processes and ensuring their inclusion is crucial. Recognizing traditional knowledge and values alongside scientific expertise helps create policies and practices that are rooted in sustainability and the well-being of both people and nature. Collaborative efforts between different stakeholders, including governments, indigenous representatives, and environmental organizations, must be fostered to establish shared visions and transformative changes.

***

THE ARCTIC'S SIGNIFICANCE in global discussions on inequality and environmental justice cannot be overstated. Understanding the complex interplay between historical legacies, climate change, and political dynamics is essential for formulating effective strategies for sustainable development and social resilience. The issues explored in this chapter provide a foundation for continued research, critical dialogue, and the development of inclusive policies that prioritize justice and well-being for all Arctic inhabitants. By engaging with these challenges, we can pave the way towards a more equitable and environmentally conscious future in the Arctic and beyond.

- Examination of the disproportionate impact of climate change on marginalized communities

As we delve into a closer examination of the disproportionate impact of climate change on marginalized communities, we begin to uncover a complex web of intersecting factors that intensify the vulnerability of these groups. The effects of climate change are felt on a global scale, but it is the most marginalized and impoverished communities that are often hit the hardest.

One key factor contributing to this unequal burden is the geographical location of marginalized communities. Many of these groups are clustered in areas that are more prone to natural disasters and extreme weather events. For example, low-income neighborhoods are often situated in floodplains, coastal regions, or areas with unstable terrain. As climate change amplifies the occurrence and intensity of events such as hurricanes, floods, and wildfires, these vulnerable communities bear the brunt of the devastation, suffering immense property damage, displacement, and loss of livelihoods.

Poverty and lack of resources further exacerbate the impact of climate change on marginalized communities. Limited financial means and infrastructural deficiencies make it difficult for these groups to adapt and recover from climate-related disasters. In many cases, marginalized communities lack access to proper housing, adequate healthcare, and essential facilities like reliable transport and clean water. When climate-related disasters strike, they are left without the necessary resources to rebuild their lives, resulting in long-term vulnerability and displacement.

Another critical factor to consider is the social determinants of health within these communities. Studies consistently show that marginalized communities face higher rates of pre-existing health conditions, such as respiratory illnesses and cardiovascular diseases, which can be exacerbated by climate change. Exposure to air pollution, extreme temperatures, and increased prevalence of disease vectors like mosquitoes and ticks all contribute to a disproportionate health burden on these communities. Additionally, limited access to healthcare and healthcare disparities further compound the adverse health effects of climate change on marginalized groups.

Displacement and forced migration are common consequences of climate change impacts on marginalized communities. When people are forced to leave their homes due to the loss of livelihoods, property damage, or unsafe living conditions, they face a myriad of challenges in finding new communities to settle in. They often encounter discrimination, prejudice, and cultural barriers, making integration into new areas challenging. This displacement can lead to diminishing social networks, loss of cultural heritage, and deep psychological trauma.

It is crucial to recognize the intersectional nature of climate change impacts on marginalized communities. Indigenous peoples, racial and ethnic minorities, women, and other socially marginalized groups face overlapping disadvantages that amplify the risks they face from climate change. Historical and ongoing systemic injustices such as discrimination, racial segregation, and economic disparities create a layered vulnerability that compounds the effects of climate change. Acknowledging and addressing these intersecting vulnerabilities is crucial to ensuring an equitable response and building resilience in these communities.

Efforts to address these challenges require a multifaceted and integrated approach. Policymakers need to prioritize the voices and needs of marginalized communities in decision-making processes, providing them with platforms to actively participate in climate governance. Economic opportunities must be created that enable these communities to transition to sustainable livelihoods. Investments in renewable energy and green infrastructure can help create jobs and mitigate the environmental degradation that disproportionately impacts marginalized communities.

Education and awareness campaigns are also vital tools in addressing the disproportionate impact of climate change. Empowering marginalized communities with knowledge about climate change, its implications, and adaptation strategies can enable them to make informed decisions and advocate for their rights.

Lastly, fostering an inclusive and intersectional environmental movement is crucial. Centering the experiences and perspectives of marginalized groups not only validates their lived realities but also highlights the importance of addressing climate change as a matter of social justice. Solidarity and collaboration across various social movements can amplify collective voices and exert pressure on governments and institutions to address the disproportionate impacts of climate change.

In conclusion, the examination of the disproportionate impact of climate change on marginalized communities reveals a stark reality of vulnerability, disparities, and social injustices. Recognizing and addressing these inequities are essential in building resilient communities that can withstand the growing challenges of our changing climate. Urgent action is needed at all levels, from grassroots initiatives to global policy frameworks, to ensure that no one is left behind in the fight against climate change.

- Analysis of the social, economic, and political factors exacerbating inequality

In recent years, the issue of inequality has become increasingly prominent in discussions surrounding social, economic, and political spheres. This exacerbation of inequality can be attributed to a variety of factors, ranging from socio-cultural to economic and political.

One of the key social factors exacerbating inequality is the perpetuation of social norms and attitudes that reinforce discrimination and prejudice. These norms, often deeply ingrained in society, result in marginalized groups facing barriers in accessing education, healthcare, and economic opportunities. For example, women and minority groups still face disproportionate levels of discrimination in the work environment, hindering their advancement and perpetuating income inequality.

Additionally, the unequal distribution of resources and wealth is a significant driving force behind economic inequality. The concentration of wealth in the hands of a few, often due to political connections or inheritance, creates a cycle of economic disparity. These individuals amass significant wealth, leaving the rest of society struggling to secure basic necessities. Lack of access to quality education and healthcare further compounds economic inequality, as individuals from disadvantaged backgrounds are less likely to achieve upward mobility.

Political factors also play a substantial role in perpetuating inequality. Oftentimes, political systems can be manipulated by the elite to consolidate power and influence policy to benefit themselves, at the expense of the majority. This can be seen through the influence of money in politics, where corporations and wealthy individuals can donate substantial amounts to finance political campaigns, effectively tilting policies in their favor. This exacerbates income inequality as policies typically cater to the interests of those in power rather than addressing the needs of the general population.

Moreover, the devaluation and limited representation of marginalized voices in decision-making processes contribute to the perpetuation of inequality. When policies are primarily crafted by individuals who are inherently privileged, it often fails to address the diverse needs of different socio-economic groups. Decision-makers need to actively include marginalized individuals and incorporate their experiences in policy-making to tackle the roots of inequality.

In conclusion, the exacerbation of social, economic, and political factors has led to the sustained growth of inequality. Tackling this issue requires addressing social norms that perpetuate discrimination, ensuring equitable distribution of resources, and constructing political systems that prioritize the needs of the majority. By addressing these factors, societies can progress towards a more inclusive and equal society where every individual has equitable access to resources, opportunities, and representation.

- Discussion on the need for equitable environmental policies and resource allocation

There is a growing recognition among global leaders and international organizations that our planet is facing significant environmental challenges. From climate change and deforestation to pollution and overexploitation of natural resources, these issues not only threaten our ecosystems but also have profound social and economic consequences.

In addressing these environmental challenges, it is essential to ensure that policies and resource allocation are conducted in an equitable manner. This means that all individuals and communities, regardless of their socio-economic status or geographical location, should have equal opportunities to access and benefit from environmental resources and services. Unfortunately, the current state of affairs often falls short of this principle.

One key reason why equitable environmental policies and resource allocation are crucial is their impact on vulnerable populations. It is well-documented that marginalized communities, including indigenous peoples, low-income groups, and racial minorities, bear a disproportionate burden of environmental harm. They often live in close proximity to polluting industries, experience limited access to clean water and air, and are most vulnerable to the impact of extreme weather events.

Without equitable policies and resource allocation, these already disadvantaged communities will have little chance of escaping the vicious cycle of poverty and environmental degradation. This perpetuates existing inequalities and hampers efforts towards sustainable development. Acknowledging and addressing the unequal distribution of environmental harms and benefits is thus fundamental to achieving social, economic, and environmental justice.

Moreover, equitable environmental policies and resource allocation can contribute to the overall efficiency and effectiveness of environmental conservation efforts. By actively involving a diverse range of stakeholders, including marginalized communities, in decision-making processes, policies can benefit from a wider variety of perspectives and knowledge. This can lead to more holistic and context-specific solutions, avoiding potential negative impacts that might arise from top-down approaches.

In addition, promoting equitable access to environmental resources such as fresh water, arable land, and clean energy can also foster long-term sustainability. By ensuring that these resources are not concentrated in the hands of a few, societies can cultivate resilience and reduce the risk of conflicts over scarce resources. Equitable resource allocation also encourages responsible consumption patterns and discourages overexploitation, as stakeholders have a vested interest in preserving the resource for future generations.

Nevertheless, attaining equitable environmental policies and resource allocation poses significant challenges. First and foremost, it requires strong political will from governments and international bodies to integrate principles of equity into their decision-making processes. This means going beyond simply addressing economic growth or environmental concerns and actively considering the needs and perspectives of marginalized communities.

Second, effective policymaking requires conducting comprehensive and participatory assessments of the social and economic impacts of environmental decisions. By involving affected communities and considering their unique circumstances, policymakers can better understand and address the distributional consequences of their actions. This necessitates building capacity and enhancing the representation of marginalized groups in the policymaking process.

Lastly, equitable environmental policies and resource allocation demand international cooperation and collaboration. Many environmental challenges, such as climate change, do not respect geographical or political borders. Therefore, efforts to achieve equity must transcend national boundaries and involve the sharing of expertise, technology, and financial resources. This calls for greater solidarity and partnership among nations and a commitment to achieving common goals.

In conclusion, promoting equitable environmental policies and resource allocation is not only a matter of justice and fairness but also a key prerequisite for environmental sustainability. By ensuring that all individuals and communities have equal opportunities to access and benefit from environmental resources, we can create resilient and prosperous societies that are capable of addressing the environmental challenges we face. Through strong political will, comprehensive assessments, and international cooperation, we can move towards a more equitable and sustainable future.

- Exploration of initiatives aiming to empower and support vulnerable populations

Currently, numerous initiatives are being implemented worldwide to empower and support vulnerable populations. These initiatives focus on key areas such as education, healthcare, employment, and social welfare, with the aim of ensuring that marginalized groups have access to resources and opportunities that can improve their quality of life.

One prominent initiative is the provision of educational opportunities for vulnerable populations. Many organizations and governments have launched programs that offer scholarships, vocational training, and mentorship to individuals from disadvantaged backgrounds. This not only equips them with practical skills but also boosts their confidence and provides them with a sense of hope for a better future. Furthermore, initiatives like after-school programs and adult literacy classes aim to bridge the education gap and reduce inequalities among vulnerable populations.

Healthcare is another crucial aspect that requires attention. Vulnerable populations often face barriers in accessing quality healthcare services. In response, initiatives have been established to provide free or low-cost healthcare to those in need. Mobile health clinics, for instance, bring medical services directly to remote and underserved areas, ensuring that everyone has access to healthcare irrespective of their location. In addition, mental health initiatives have been introduced to address the specific psychological challenges faced by vulnerable populations, providing them with the necessary support and therapy.

Employment opportunities are essential for breaking the cycle of poverty and vulnerability. Initiatives promoting skills development and entrepreneurship training have been introduced to help marginalized individuals secure stable and sustainable employment. Microfinance initiatives, for example, provide small loans to individuals who lack access to traditional banking institutions, enabling them to start their own small businesses.

Collaboration between governments, private sector entities, and NGOs is often crucial in these initiatives, as it maximizes resources and expertise to support vulnerable populations.

Critically, social welfare initiatives play a vital role in empowering vulnerable populations by providing them with access to basic necessities and safety nets. Food security programs, for example, aim to ensure that no individual goes hungry by distributing nutritious meals or providing food vouchers to the needy. Furthermore, programs addressing housing insecurity and homelessness seek to provide shelter and support for those without adequate housing. These initiatives also often foster social inclusion, offering counseling services or community engagement programs to meet the diverse needs of vulnerable populations.

In evaluating the progress of these initiatives, it is crucial to consider the contextual factors that may impact their effectiveness. Cultural, political, and socio-economic factors can either facilitate or hinder the implementation and sustainability of empowerment and support projects. Recognizing and addressing these challenges is vital to ensure that vulnerable populations truly benefit from these initiatives.

In conclusion, the exploration of initiatives aiming to empower and support vulnerable populations reveals an array of strategies that address fundamental needs such as education, healthcare, employment, and social welfare. These initiatives not only provide immediate support but also aim to secure long-term empowerment for marginalized groups. However, ongoing collaboration and continuous evaluation are critical to ensure that these initiatives remain effective, adaptable, and inclusive, creating a stronger and more resilient future for vulnerable populations.

Chapter 13: Losses and Gains: Balancing Environmental Challenges and Opportunities

In this chapter, we delve into the complex task of navigating environmental challenges while also seizing the opportunities that come with it. The world we live in today is constantly changing and evolving, placing increasing pressures on our environment. As a result, it has become imperative for us to strike a delicate balance between mitigating losses and capitalizing on gains.

One of the major challenges we face is the loss of biodiversity. Human activities such as deforestation, pollution, and climate change have resulted in the decline of various species worldwide. The loss of biodiversity not only disrupts ecosystems but also threatens our own well-being. In this chapter, we explore the ways in which we can halt this loss by implementing conservation measures, strengthening environmental legislation, and fostering sustainable practices.

Another significant challenge we address is climate change. The burning of fossil fuels, among other human activities, has led to the increase in greenhouse gases in our atmosphere, resulting in global warming and its wide-ranging consequences. From rising sea levels to extreme weather events, climate change poses a grave threat to both natural and human systems. However, amidst this gloom, there are opportunities to be seized. Through the transition to clean and renewable energy sources, the reduction of emissions, and the adoption of sustainable practices, we can not only minimize the loss caused by climate change but also create a more environmentally friendly and economically viable future.

Moreover, in this chapter, we explore the delicate balance required in managing natural resources. As the demand for resources continually grows, we are faced with the need to extract more from the Earth. However, this pursuit of resources should be done responsibly and sustainably to minimize negative impacts. By implementing practices such as resource conservation, recycling, and embracing the principles of the circular economy, we can achieve a balance where we meet our needs without compromising the ability of future generations to meet theirs.

Additionally, we discuss the importance of biodiversity conservation, not only for the sake of nature but also for human well-being. Many ecosystems provide essential services, including clean air and water, regulated climate, and nutrient cycling. By protecting and restoring these ecosystems, we can simultaneously ensure the well-being of both nature and society. Moreover, we explore the concept of ecosystem-based approaches, where we recognize the interconnectedness of human and natural systems and aim to manage them as a whole. This holistic approach allows us to minimize losses while leveraging the gains that come from healthy and functioning ecosystems.

Furthermore, we delve into the role of technology and innovation in achieving a balance between environmental challenges and opportunities. Breakthroughs in technology have immense potential to drive positive change and facilitate sustainable development. From renewable energy technologies to innovative farming practices, we explore how these advancements can help us address the challenges we face. However, it is crucial to ensure that these technologies are utilized responsibly and ethically, taking into consideration potential unintended consequences and ensuring equitable access for all.

In conclusion, this chapter provides a comprehensive overview of the losses and gains associated with environmental challenges. It is through a thoughtful and balanced approach that we can mitigate losses, seize opportunities, and build a resilient and sustainable future. By taking proactive steps towards conservation, resource management, and adoption of sustainable practices, we can not only safeguard our environment but also unlock the enormous potential for economic growth and social well-being.

- Examination of the conflicting interests between economic development and environmental protection

Examination of the Conflicting Interests between Economic Development and Environmental Protection

AS HUMAN SOCIETIES continue to progress and expand, the age-old conflict between economic development and environmental protection becomes increasingly critical. Economic development aims to enhance the standards of living, alleviate poverty, and drive overall prosperity through industrialization and increasing production. On the other hand, environmental protection seeks to conserve natural resources, prevent pollution, and preserve ecosystems for the long-term well-being of our planet and future generations. This essay explores the intricate relationship, inherent conflicts, and possible solutions that arise when economic development and environmental protection clash.

Intrinsic Conflicts:

The conflicts between economic development and environmental protection can be traced back to their inherent disparities in objectives, timeframes, and priorities. Economic development, driven by political and social pressures, often requires the utilization of natural resources at an accelerated pace. This process depletes non-renewable resources, damages ecosystems, and increases pollution, thus compromising environmental sustainability. Meanwhile, environmental protection urges restraint, conservation, and the adoption of sustainable practices, often leading to perceived limitations on economic growth and slower progress.

Among the areas where these conflicting interests are most apparent is in the development and expansion of industries that heavily rely on finite natural resources. For instance, mining for minerals and fossil fuels contributes significantly to economic growth but also leads to irreversible damage to ecosystems, soil erosion, and water contamination. Similarly, large-scale agriculture and deforestation for expansion reduce biodiversity and disrupt natural habitats, leading to compromised ecosystems and reduced freshwater availability.

Moreover, economic development often necessitates increased energy production, leading to a rise in greenhouse gas emissions, air pollution, and climate change. Balancing the energy requirements to power industries with the need to protect the environment imposes a constant challenge. Expanding fossil fuel-based energy sources contribute to economic growth but exacerbate environmental degradation, posing long-term risks to public health and ecological balance.

Potential Solutions:

Adopting a holistic approach that seeks to strike a sustainable balance between economic development and environmental protection is essential to address these conflicts. Toward this end, several potential solutions can be considered:

1. Integration of Sustainable Development practices: Policymakers should explore alternative models of development that prioritize sustainability, with the aim of minimizing resource consumption, waste generation, and environmental impact. By investing in renewable energy sources, green technologies, and sustainable agriculture practices, we can mitigate the negative impact of economic growth on our environment.

2. Regulatory Measures and Economic Incentives: Governments and international organizations must implement strict environmental regulations, imposing penalties for non-compliance, while simultaneously ensuring incentives for adopting environmentally friendly practices. By internalizing the costs of environmental damage and pollution, industries can be encouraged to move towards more sustainable methods of production and minimize their ecological footprint.

3. Collaborative Approaches: Stakeholders from both economic and environmental domains should engage in a collaborative dialogue to find common ground and identify mutually beneficial solutions. Encouraging cooperation between industries, conservationists, local communities, and governments can lead to more inclusive decision-making processes and better

policy outcomes, ensuring both economic growth and environmental protection.

4. Education and Awareness: Promoting environmental education at all levels is crucial in fostering a culture of sustainable thinking and action. By increasing public awareness about the interconnectedness of economic development and environmental protection, individuals can make informed choices and pressure policymakers to prioritize sustainability considerations.

———◉———

THE CONFLICTS BETWEEN economic development and environmental protection continue to pose immense challenges. Striking a balance between these seemingly opposing forces requires a paradigm shift in the way we perceive development and its relationship with the environment. While economic growth is essential for human progress, it should not come at the expense of the ecological systems that sustain life on our planet. Through a concerted effort, inclusive policies, and cooperative decision-making, it is possible to reconcile these conflicting interests and build a more sustainable future where economic development and environmental protection coexist harmoniously.

- Analysis of the potential trade-offs and benefits associated with Arctic warming

Arctic warming, a consequence of anthropogenic climate change, presents a range of potential trade-offs and benefits that can have far-reaching implications for the environment, Indigenous communities, and global economies. Understanding these trade-offs and benefits is crucial for forming effective strategies for adapting to and mitigating the impacts of Arctic warming.

One of the main trade-offs associated with Arctic warming is the loss of valuable ecosystems and biodiversity. The Arctic region is home to unique and fragile ecosystems, such as polar ice caps, tundra, and Arctic marine environments. As the area warms, these ecosystems are under threat, with melting ice caps and permafrost degradation leading to habitat loss and species displacement. This loss of biodiversity not only disrupts natural ecological processes but also has implications for food chains and nutrient cycles that sustain indigenous wildlife and human populations, such as the Inuit.

On the other hand, there are also potential benefits to Arctic warming that cannot be ignored. One of the major advantages is the opening up of new shipping routes and increased accessibility to previously inaccessible natural resources. The shrinking of ice caps allows for increased shipping activity in the Arctic Ocean, which is shorter and more cost-effective for transit between Europe and Asia. Additionally, the Arctic holds vast reserves of oil, natural gas, minerals, and other resources that were once financially and technically prohibited from extraction due to the harsh climate. The exploitation of these resources could bring economic opportunities and development to Arctic nations and possibly reduce dependence on other regions for resources.

Nevertheless, it is crucial to evaluate these potential benefits in light of their environmental and social consequences. Increased shipping activity in the Arctic poses risks to marine ecosystems and indigenous livelihoods dependent on fishing and hunting. The extraction of resources in a fragile and previously untouched environment can lead to habitat destruction, pollution, and further exacerbation of climate change. Moreover, any economic benefits derived from Arctic resource exploitation need to be weighed against sustainability concerns and long-term impacts.

Furthermore, Arctic warming poses global concerns related to climate feedback loops. The melting of Arctic sea ice exposes darker ocean surfaces, which absorb more solar radiation, exacerbating global warming. This positive feedback loop can lead to accelerated climate change, with impacts felt globally, such as sea-level rise, extreme weather events, and disruptions to ocean currents and heat transport. The potential trade-offs of exploiting Arctic resources and taking advantage of shipping routes need to be considered alongside these overall global climate risks.

In summary, the trade-offs and benefits associated with Arctic warming are complex and interconnected. While it offers new opportunities for shipping and resource extraction, this comes at the cost of irreversible habitat loss, biodiversity decline, and exacerbating global climate change. Careful and sustainable management is required to maximize potential benefits while minimizing negative impacts, ensuring the survival of Arctic ecosystems, and protecting the cultural and economic interests of indigenous populations. Analysis and understanding of these potential trade-offs and benefits are essential for informed decision-making and effective climate change mitigation and adaptation strategies.

- Discussion on the ethics of resource exploitation in the vulnerable Arctic ecosystem

Resource exploitation in the vulnerable Arctic ecosystem is a topic that has sparked much debate and discussion in recent years. The region is home to unique ecosystems and a delicate balance of biodiversity that is highly susceptible to human interference. As the Arctic ice continues to melt at alarming rates due to climate change, this once largely untouched expanse is becoming increasingly accessible for various forms of resource exploitation, such as oil drilling, mining, and commercial fishing.

One of the primary ethical concerns surrounding resource exploitation in the Arctic is the potential for irreversible environmental damage. The delicate ecosystems found in this region are often slow to recover from disturbances, and any disturbances caused by human activities could have long-lasting effects. For example, oil spills have resulted in devastating consequences for the marine environments in the past, and an Arctic oil spill could be catastrophic for the local wildlife and communities that depend on these ecosystems for their livelihoods.

Additionally, the extraction and exploitation of resources in the Arctic often involve the use of heavy machinery, carbon emissions, and other pollutants that contribute to climate change. This represents a significant ethical dilemma, as the exploitation of resources in this fragile region contributes to the very problem- global warming- that is already threatening its existence. By further exacerbating climate change through Arctic resource exploitation, we risk causing a domino effect of environmental damage that could have consequences far beyond the immediate area.

Furthermore, the Arctic region is home to indigenous communities that have historically relied on its resources for their subsistence and cultural practices. These communities have unique and valuable knowledge systems built over generations, allowing them to sustainably manage the resources within this environment. The ethics of resource exploitation in the Arctic should consider the rights and well-being of these indigenous communities, as their cultural heritage and ways of life could be severely impacted by the extractive activities of resource companies.

On the other hand, some argue that resource exploitation in the Arctic can bring economic opportunities to the region and its inhabitants, potentially increasing their standard of living. The extractive industries can create jobs, boost local economies, and provide revenue for governments. However, this argument must be tempered by a balanced consideration of the potential environmental consequences and the long-term sustainability of these economic benefits.

In order to ensure a more ethical approach to resource exploitation in the Arctic, several measures can be considered. Firstly, robust environmental impact assessments must be conducted before any new projects are approved, taking into account both short-term and long-term effects. Furthermore, effective regulations and safeguards should be put in place to minimize the risk of accidents and ensure the responsibility of resource extraction companies in case of any environmental harm.

In addition, indigenous communities must be involved in the decision-making process concerning resource exploitation and their traditional knowledge should be recognized and integrated into any development plans. Their consent and participation in discussions about resource extraction should be respected, and they should be fairly compensated for the potential negative impacts on their way of life.

Finally, a shift towards sustainable and renewable energy sources must be considered as a long-term solution. Investing in clean technologies, reducing greenhouse gas emissions, and working towards a more sustainable future will not only protect the vulnerable Arctic ecosystem but also contribute to the global fight against climate change.

In conclusion, the discussions on the ethics of resource exploitation in the Arctic must navigate the fine line between economic opportunities and environmental preservation. Proper environmental assessments, recognition of indigenous knowledge and rights, and a commitment to sustainability are all necessary to mitigate the potentially irreversible damage to this already vulnerable ecosystem. Only by approaching resource exploitation in a responsible and ethical manner can we safeguard the Arctic for future generations.

- Evaluation of strategies to achieve a sustainable balance in the Arctic region

The Arctic region is a unique and fragile ecosystem that is facing numerous challenges due to climate change and human activities. Achieving a sustainable balance in this region requires the development and implementation of effective strategies that address environmental, economic, and social concerns.

One strategy to achieve a sustainable balance in the Arctic is the promotion of renewable energy sources. As the Arctic experiences melting ice and shrinking permafrost, there is increased potential for the exploitation of renewable energy resources such as solar, wind, and geothermal power. Investing in these sources can help reduce greenhouse gas emissions, decrease reliance on fossil fuels, and promote sustainable development in the region.

Another strategy is the implementation of sustainable and responsible resource extraction practices. The Arctic is known for its abundance of natural resources, including oil, gas, and minerals. However, extraction of these resources can have adverse impacts on the environment, wildlife, and indigenous communities. Implementing strict regulations and guidelines for resource extraction, such as sustainable mining practices and responsible oil drilling techniques, can help mitigate these impacts and ensure long-term sustainability.

Preservation and conservation of Arctic ecosystems is also a crucial strategy. The Arctic is home to unique and vulnerable species, such as polar bears, Arctic foxes, and beluga whales. Protecting their habitats and ensuring their survival should be a priority. This can be achieved through the creation of protected areas, biodiversity conservation efforts, and sustainable tourism practices. By preserving the Arctic's ecosystems, we can maintain its ecological balance and promote sustainable tourism activities that generate economic benefits for local communities.

In addition to these strategies, effective governance and international cooperation are key factors in achieving a sustainable balance in the Arctic. The Arctic comprises multiple countries, each with its own interests, policies, and priorities. Cooperation and collaboration among these nations is essential to address common challenges, establish guidelines for sustainable development, and protect the rights and interests of indigenous communities. International agreements and organizations like the Arctic Council play a vital role in facilitating these collaborations and ensuring effective governance.

Furthermore, engaging and involving indigenous communities in decision-making processes is crucial for achieving a sustainable balance in the Arctic. Indigenous peoples have a deep understanding of the region's ecology, and their traditional knowledge can offer important insights and solutions to environmental challenges. Establishing meaningful partnerships and consultation mechanisms with indigenous communities can help ensure that their rights, traditions, and livelihoods are respected and integrated into sustainable development strategies.

Overall, achieving a sustainable balance in the Arctic requires a multifaceted approach that incorporates renewable energy, responsible resource extraction, ecosystem preservation, effective governance, international cooperation, and indigenous participation. By implementing these strategies, we can work towards safeguarding the Arctic for future generations and ensuring its long-term environmental, economic, and social sustainability.

Chapter 14: The Role of Advocacy and Public Awareness

In today's complex and interconnected world, advocacy and public awareness play a crucial role in raising awareness, promoting change, and mobilizing collective action on a wide range of issues. This chapter aims to explore the significance of advocacy and public awareness in driving positive change, discussing their methodologies, and evaluating their impact.

Advocacy: Empowering Voices for Change

Advocacy can be defined as the process of empowering individuals or groups to raise their voices, express their concerns, and mobilize support for a cause or issue that they believe in. It is an essential tool for promoting and achieving social justice, human rights, gender equality, environmental sustainability, healthcare access, education, poverty eradication, and numerous other societal goals.

Whether it is campaigning for policy changes, lobbying governments and institutions, or challenging social norms and structures, advocacy helps provide a platform for marginalized voices and promotes inclusivity and diversity. It enables citizens to engage in participatory democracy, making governance more accountable and responsive to the needs and aspirations of the people.

Advocacy Strategies and Tactics

Advocacy employs a range of strategies and tactics to bring about change effectively. These include grassroots mobilization, community organizing, media campaigns, social media activism, petitioning, protests, engagement with policymakers, and more. By employing a combination of these strategies, advocates can influence public opinion, compel decision-makers to take action, and push for meaningful and sustainable policy changes.

Public Awareness: Shaping Perception and Behavior

Public awareness campaigns are designed to build knowledge and understanding among the general public about specific issues, challenges, or causes. Often driven by advocacy organizations, non-profits, and governmental entities, these campaigns aim to shape public opinion and foster positive attitudes, ultimately leading to changes in behavior and social norms.

Public awareness initiatives utilize various communication tools such as mass media campaigns, educational programs, social media engagement, documentary films, and art campaigns. These aim to inform and educate the public about widespread issues like climate change, discrimination, mental health, sexual and reproductive health rights, and more. By creating empathy, understanding, and promoting shared values, public awareness campaigns can galvanize individuals and communities to take action and support advocacy efforts.

Impact and Evaluation

The impact of advocacy and public awareness campaigns can be challenging to measure quantitatively. Still, qualitative indicators such as policy changes, increased public support, improved legislation, shifts in public opinion, and enhanced awareness can help evaluate their effectiveness.

Case studies and success stories from various advocacy campaigns can provide valuable insights into the power of public awareness and advocacy to bring about change. Looking at examples like the civil rights movement, the campaign for marriage equality, anti-apartheid movement, and environmental activism, it becomes evident how sustained efforts, combined with strategic advocacy and effective public awareness, can reshape societies, laws, and institutions.

⎯⎯◉⎯⎯

ADVOCACY AND PUBLIC awareness remain indispensable tools for addressing pressing global challenges and promoting social progress. By amplifying voices, influencing policy, generating support, and shaping public attitudes and behaviors, advocacy and public awareness campaigns can lay the foundation for a more just, inclusive, and sustainable world. As we move forward, it is crucial for individuals, organizations, and governments to recognize the importance of utilizing these powerful tools and work towards amplifying collective action for meaningful change.

- Importance of raising awareness and mobilizing collective action

Raising awareness and mobilizing collective action are vital aspects of addressing various societal issues and creating positive change. It involves educating individuals about specific problems, highlighting their importance, and encouraging them to take action collectively. The aim is to increase people's understanding, build empathy, and motivate them to actively engage in finding solutions. Whether tackling environmental concerns, social injustices, or public health crises, raising awareness and mobilizing collective action play a significant role in effecting real and lasting transformation.

First and foremost, raising awareness is crucial because it informs individuals about pressing issues that might otherwise go unnoticed or overlooked. People are often busy with their lives, and without knowledge of certain problems, they may not feel compelled to take action. Raising awareness throws a spotlight on these concerns and fosters understanding, making people aware of the impact they can have in addressing the issue at hand. For instance, campaigns or initiatives to combat climate change seek to educate individuals about the devastating consequences of global warming, ultimately encouraging them to adopt sustainable practices, reduce greenhouse gas emissions, or advocate for policy changes.

Furthermore, raising awareness creates solidarity amongst individuals who share common concerns. By highlighting the existence of a problem and the need for collective action, people who may have felt isolated or powerless now have an opportunity to connect with like-minded individuals and organizations. This sense of unity provides a platform for collaboration, sparking dialogue, and inspiring collective efforts towards finding innovative solutions. For instance, movements like Black Lives Matter have successfully raised awareness about racial injustices, bringing people together to voice their concerns, demand change, and work towards dismantling systemic racism.

Additionally, mobilizing collective action is vital because it leverages collective power to drive change. When individuals come together, the impact of their efforts can be amplified significantly. Collaborative initiatives allow for the pooling of resources, talent, and skills to tackle complex problems effectively. By mobilizing a collective force, groups can accomplish more than what individuals acting alone could achieve. For example, medical professionals, community leaders, and volunteers collaborated during the COVID-19 pandemic to raise awareness about preventive measures, support the overwhelmed healthcare system, and advocate for equitable vaccine distribution.

Moreover, raising awareness and mobilizing collective action strengthen democratic processes and civic engagement. Informed and engaged citizens play a critical role in holding governments and institutions accountable. By advocating for policy changes, participating in protests, or supporting grassroots organizations, individuals can influence decision-making processes and amplify marginalized voices. Raising awareness fosters a sense of citizenship and empowers people to actively assert their rights, shaping the ethical and moral fabric of a society.

In conclusion, the importance of raising awareness and mobilizing collective action should not be underestimated. It serves as a catalyst for change by educating individuals, fostering solidarity, leveraging collective power, and strengthening democratic processes. Renowned changemakers, activists, and organizations recognize the significance of creating awareness and mobilizing collective action to address various societal issues effectively. By engaging individuals and inspiring collective efforts, we can bring about positive and sustainable change for humanity and the planet.

- Examination of successful advocacy campaigns and initiatives

Advocacy campaigns and initiatives have often played a crucial role in bringing about positive change in various spheres of society. By drawing attention to important issues, mobilizing support, and pushing for policy reforms, successful advocacy efforts have achieved significant milestones and impacted countless lives. In this examination, we will delve into some of the most poignant and effective advocacy campaigns and initiatives across different domains.

One exemplary advocacy campaign that deserves recognition is the civil rights movement in the United States, particularly its fight against racial segregation and discrimination in the mid-20th century. Led by influential figures such as Martin Luther King Jr. and Rosa Parks, this movement utilized peaceful protests, marches, and boycotts to raise awareness and demand equal rights for African Americans. Through their tireless efforts, they successfully pushed for landmark legislation like the Civil Rights Act of 1964 and the Voting Rights Act of 1965, dismantling institutionalized racism and paving the way for greater equality.

Another noteworthy campaign occurred in the environmental sector, with the international movement against climate change spearheaded by organizations like Greenpeace and individuals such as Al Gore. Their goal was to address the urgent issue of global warming and dwindling natural resources. Through grassroots organizing, advocacy campaigns, and comprehensive communication strategies, they raised awareness about the consequences of climate change and pressured governments to prioritize sustainable policies. As a result, international agreements like the Paris Agreement were reached, committing countries to reducing greenhouse gas emissions and transitioning to low-carbon economies.

In the field of human rights, the campaign for LGBTQ+ rights has witnessed remarkable progress recently. Advocacy groups like the Human

Rights Campaign and Stonewall have played a pivotal role in changing societal attitudes and promoting legal reforms. Strategies such as storytelling, education, and lobbying have been employed to address discrimination and secure equal rights for the LGBTQ+ community. Significant milestones, including the legalization of same-sex marriage in various countries and the implementation of anti-discrimination laws, have been achieved due to these dedicated advocacy efforts.

Moreover, the healthcare sector has also seen successful advocacy campaigns bring about transformative changes. One notable initiative is the global movement for access to essential medicines, where organizations like Médecins Sans Frontières (Doctors Without Borders) have been at the forefront. They have fought to ensure that life-saving medications are affordable and available to all, particularly in developing countries. Public awareness campaigns, patent law reforms, and grassroots activism have contributed to significant progress in making crucial drugs more accessible to vulnerable populations worldwide.

These exemplary advocacy campaigns and initiatives share some common factors that have contributed to their success. Firstly, they effectively utilized various communication channels to engage and mobilize their target audiences, including traditional media, social media, and direct engagement with policymakers. Additionally, these campaigns recognized the importance of fostering partnerships and alliances with like-minded organizations, harnessing collective power and resources to amplify their impact. Furthermore, they consistently employed evidence-based arguments and storytelling techniques to make their case relatable and compelling, resonating with a broad range of stakeholders.

In conclusion, successful advocacy campaigns and initiatives have indelibly shaped our society, leading to significant progress across diverse areas. From civil rights to environmental conservation, from LGBTQ+ rights to access to healthcare, these campaigns have harnessed the power of communication, strategic partnerships, and evidence-based advocacy to effect change. By examining their strategies, approaches, and outcomes, we can learn valuable lessons for future advocacy efforts, ensuring that our world becomes a better place for all.

- Discussion on the role of media, education, and public engagement

In today's society, the role of media, education, and public engagement is crucial in shaping the way people think, consume information, and participate in social, political, and cultural discussions. These three elements not only have the power to inform and educate but also to influence public opinion, enabling us to shape our worldview and contribute to the development of informed societies.

Media plays a significant role in broadcasting and distributing information to the public. It serves as a bridge between what is happening around the world and the individuals who seek knowledge. Whether it is through traditional forms of media like newspapers, television channels, or radio, or through more contemporary platforms like social media, the media has the ability to shape public discourse by highlighting and amplifying certain messages or stories. This unique power comes with a great responsibility to ensure that information is accurate, objective, and balanced. However, media transparency and credibility sometimes face challenges due to biases, sensationalism, and pressure from external interests. Therefore, it is crucial for media outlets to strive for unbiased reporting and encourage critical thinking among their audiences to foster an informed citizenry.

Education plays a vital role in disseminating knowledge, providing individuals with a strong foundation to understand complex issues, engage in informed discussions, and make rational decisions. By equipping students with various subjects and skills, education acts as an empowering tool, enabling individuals to navigate the world around them and make independent judgments. This includes teaching students how to critically analyze media, spot misinformation, and engage with sources responsibly. However, educational institutions should also promote a diverse range of opinions, as exposure to different perspectives facilitates open-mindedness and tolerance. Encouraging debate and discussions in classrooms helps individuals develop their analytical skills, learn to respect diverse opinions, and participate actively in shaping societal dialogues.

Public engagement is a fundamental aspect of democratic societies, as it empowers individuals to voice their concerns, contribute to policy discussions, and hold decision-makers accountable. When citizens are actively engaged in politics, social movements, or community initiatives, they foster a participatory democracy that reflects the needs and aspirations of its people. Media and education play complementary roles in facilitating effective public engagement. Media serves as a platform to raise awareness about pertinent issues, highlight grassroots movements, and provide a space for those who might otherwise struggle to make their voices heard. Meanwhile, education helps individuals develop critical thinking skills, empathy, and the ability to analyze complex situations from various perspectives. By using the knowledge gained through education and the platform provided by media, individuals can participate in public discussions and influence decision-making processes.

It is essential to acknowledge the interdependence of media, education, and public engagement in order to develop an informed and engaged citizenry. All three elements rely on each other for their effectiveness and have the potential to be powerful tools in shaping the future of our society. By promoting media literacy, fostering critical thinking skills, and encouraging active public participation, we can create a society that is well-informed, engaged, and empowered to tackle the challenges of the present and contribute to a brighter future.

- Analysis of the challenges and opportunities in fostering a global climate-conscious society

Analysis of Challenges and Opportunities in Fostering a Global Climate-Conscious Society

CLIMATE CHANGE IS ONE of the greatest challenges facing humanity today, and solutions require a coordinated effort on a global scale. Creating a climate-conscious society is crucial for achieving the necessary reductions in greenhouse gas emissions and promoting sustainable development. This analysis examines the challenges and opportunities in fostering a global climate-conscious society, aiming to provide insights into crucial areas that need attention and ways to harness opportunities.

Challenges:

1. Lack of Awareness and Education:

One significant challenge is the limited understanding of climate change and its impacts. Many individuals, particularly in developing countries, lack awareness of the issue's urgency and the actions necessary to mitigate and adapt to it. Bridging this knowledge gap through educational programs and awareness campaigns is essential to fostering a climate-conscious society.

2. Political Will and Multilateral Collaboration:

Addressing climate change requires global political will and multilateral collaboration. This challenge is particularly evident in international negotiations where competing national interests often overshadow cooperative efforts. Overcoming this challenge necessitates robust agreements, fostering increased collaboration, setting ambitious targets, and sharing responsibilities among nations.

3. Economic Influence and Transition Costs:

Large-scale transitions to renewable energy and sustainable practices face economic challenges. Economic powerhouses often resist change due to vested interests in fossil fuels or face concerns about job losses. Fostering a climate-conscious society requires innovative economic models that promote growth while minimizing environmental harm. Supporting sustainable business practices, green job creation, and transitioning from fossil fuel subsidies can help mitigate these economic hurdles.

4. Socio-cultural Norms and Behavioral Change:

Changing societal norms on consumption patterns and individual behavior is another hurdle. People are often resistant to adopting new habits or making necessary sacrifices as it may disrupt their comfort and routine. However, encouraging behavioral change through targeted awareness campaigns, incentives, and community-based action can gradually shift societal norms towards a climate-conscious paradigm.

Opportunities:

1. Technological Advancements:

Rapid advancements in renewable energy, energy storage, and carbon capture technologies provide significant opportunities for a low-carbon society. Embracing these innovations can reduce dependency on fossil fuels and improve overall energy efficiency. Governments and businesses should invest in research, development, and deployment to seize these growing opportunities while fostering technological exchange between nations.

2. Sustainable Urban Planning:

Rapid urbanization presents a chance to implement sustainable urban planning practices. Compact cities, efficient public transportation systems, green infrastructure, and energy-efficient buildings can mitigate carbon emissions significantly. Encouraging policies and financial incentives that promote sustainable urbanization can serve as a catalyst for widespread climate-consciousness.

3. Collaboration among Stakeholders:

Fostering a global climate-conscious society necessitates collaboration among diverse stakeholders. Governments, businesses, academia, and civil society organizations can work together to raise awareness, share best practices, and promote sustainable development. Public-private partnerships, knowledge-sharing platforms, and collaborative projects can maximize the impact of collective efforts.

4. Climate Action Integration:

Integrating climate action into various sectors, policies, and decision-making frameworks presents an opportunity to mainstream climate-consciousness. Incorporating climate change considerations into education, public health, finance, and agriculture can create a comprehensive approach. By demonstrating the practical benefits and the close link between climate action and various sectors, fostering a climate-conscious society becomes more feasible.

———◉———

FOSTERING A GLOBAL climate-conscious society is a complex and multi-faceted task. While challenges persist, there are numerous opportunities to address them effectively. Generating awareness, embracing technological advancements, promoting sustainable urban planning, and fostering collaboration are key avenues for progress. With concerted efforts and a shared global vision, society can overcome challenges and seize opportunities to create a sustainable future. It is imperative to act now to ensure a liveable planet for the current and future generations.

Chapter 15: Ethical Considerations in Climate Change

The issue of climate change is not just a scientific or environmental concern; it also has profound ethical dimensions that require careful consideration. With the increasing awareness of the negative impacts of human activities and greenhouse gas emissions on the planet, discussions surrounding climate change have expanded to include moral and ethical questions.

One of the main ethical considerations in climate change is the issue of responsibility. Who is responsible for climate change and its consequences? Is it the individuals who emit greenhouse gases through their daily activities, the businesses that contribute to pollution, or the governments that fail to implement and enforce effective climate policies? Climate change is a collective problem that requires collective responsibility, and assigning blame and responsibility is a complex and challenging task.

From an ethical perspective, developed countries that have historically contributed the most to global warming bear a greater responsibility in addressing climate change. Their higher per capita emissions and historical exploitation of natural resources have fuelled economic growth while leading to a sharp rise in greenhouse gas emissions. On the other hand, developing countries with rapidly growing economies argue that developed nations should bear the brunt of the responsibility as they have reaped the benefits of industrialization for much longer.

Another ethical consideration in climate change is intergenerational justice. The decisions and actions taken today will have far-reaching consequences for future generations. The impacts of climate change are expected to worsen over time, with rising sea levels, extreme weather events, and ecological disruptions affecting our descendants. Thus, addressing climate change ethically requires thinking beyond short-term political or economic gains and considering the interests and rights of future generations.

In addition to responsibility and intergenerational justice, distributive justice is another crucial ethical consideration in climate change. The impacts of climate change are not evenly distributed, with vulnerable communities and developing nations being disproportionately affected. Those who have contributed the least to climate change often bear the greatest burdens. Addressing this imbalance and ensuring fair access to resources and support for adaptation and resilience is essential to uphold distributive justice in climate change discussions.

Overcoming ethical challenges in climate change requires engaging in lively debates and involving diverse perspectives. Finding common ground and collective action is crucial to address this global problem effectively. Ethical considerations should inform policy decisions, guide international agreements, and shape individual actions to mitigate and adapt to climate change.

Addressing ethical considerations in climate change calls for transformative actions on multiple fronts. It involves transitioning to sustainable energy sources, encouraging sustainable consumption and production patterns, promoting the inclusion and participation of marginalized communities, supporting developing countries in adapting to climate change, and fostering international cooperation.

The ethical considerations surrounding climate change are intertwined with moral values, justice, and the well-being of both current and future generations. Solving this complex problem requires interdisciplinary and comprehensive approaches that incorporate scientific knowledge, policy making, and moral reflections. By recognizing and embracing these ethical considerations, we can collectively work towards a more sustainable and equitable future.

- Exploration of ethical dilemmas triggered by Arctic warming

The Ethical Dilemmas Triggered by Arctic Warming: A Comprehensive Exploration

AS ARCTIC WARMING ACCELERATES due to climate change, a series of ethical dilemmas has arisen in this fragile ecosystem. The consequences of melting ice caps, rising temperatures, and altering habitats extend beyond the immediate region, affecting global climate patterns and ecological balance. Exploring the ethical dimensions of these dilemmas allows us to understand the vast implications of Arctic warming and aids in formulating appropriate responses.

Ecological Balance versus Economic Interests:

Perhaps the most significant ethical dilemma surrounding Arctic warming involves the clash between environmental concerns and economic interests. The melting Arctic ice has unveiled valuable resources such as oil, natural gas, and minerals, sparking a race for exploitation. Balancing the need for economic development and safeguarding fragile ecosystems raises questions about the moral responsibilities we collectively hold towards the planet's Arctic region.

Rights of Indigenous Arctic Communities:

Decades of industrial activities and the rapid pace of climate change disrupt the traditional livelihoods of indigenous Arctic communities. These groups have longstanding cultural and historic connections in the region, making them exceptionally vulnerable to the drastic environmental changes caused by global warming. Ethical considerations underscore the need for community consultation, participation, and collaboration in decision-making processes to ensure the rights of indigenous Arctic populations are respected.

The Fate of Arctic Wildlife:

Arctic warming has dire consequences for diverse flora and fauna inhabiting the region. Species such as polar bears, seals, and various marine organisms face an uncertain future as their habitat rapidly transforms. Ethical dilemmas arise in determining how much effort society should invest in the conservation of these iconic species, acknowledging their intrinsic value as components of the world's biodiversity. Striking a balance between human development and preserving unique Arctic biodiversity becomes an ethical conundrum of global significance.

Security and Geopolitical Implications:

With the Arctic becoming increasingly navigable due to melting ice, new seaways open up, along with opportunities for resource extraction and competition among nations. Rifts between nations regarding sovereignty, natural resource claims, and navigation rights present intricate ethical dilemmas. Delicate governance structures need to be crafted to ensure cooperation, protection of shared resources, and prevent conflicts from arising as the Arctic's attractiveness grows.

The Climate Justice Imperative:

Arctic warming contributes significantly to global climate change, impacting low-lying regions and vulnerable communities worldwide. Ethically, the carbon-intensive activities in developed nations have perpetuated the unequal burden faced by developing countries disproportionately affected by climate change. Addressing this ethical issue not only involves reducing greenhouse gas emissions but also adopting a holistic approach towards climate justice, where the share of responsibilities is distributed fairly and equitably across nations.

⸻ ◉ ⸻

THE EXPLORATION OF ethical dilemmas triggered by Arctic warming reveals the profound interconnectedness between environmental, social, and economic factors. The delicate balance between ecological well-being, indigenous rights, species preservation, geopolitical stability, and climate justice necessitates a collective ethical responsibility to tackle Arctic warming's consequences.

However, ethical dilemmas can only be consciously addressed if we acknowledge the long-term environmental impact of our actions and foster sustainable practices globally. By prioritizing the protection of fragile Arctic ecosystems and ensuring the well-being of all those affected, we can pave the way toward a more equitable and sustainable future for our planet.

- Analysis of responsibilities of stakeholders, governments, and individuals

The responsibilities of stakeholders, governments, and individuals in various sectors play a crucial role in advancing societies. Each group has distinct roles and functions that contribute to the overall wellbeing and development of communities. In this analysis, we will delve into the specific responsibilities of these entities and how they interact to create an optimal environment for growth and progress.

Stakeholders, in any given context, can be defined as individuals or entities that have a direct or indirect interest in a particular area, organization, or industry. They can include business owners, investors, employees, customers, and local communities. Stakeholders have both ethical and practical responsibilities that influence the direction and impact of their involvement.

First and foremost, stakeholders are responsible for ensuring that their actions and decisions are ethical and abide by societal norms and values. They must operate in a transparent and accountable manner, taking into account the needs and expectations of the broader community. For example, business stakeholders have a responsibility to conduct their operations in an environmentally sustainable manner, considering the long-term consequences of their actions on the planet.

Moreover, stakeholders have a responsibility to contribute to the economic development and prosperity of the organization or sector they are involved in. Businesses, for instance, have a duty to create jobs, generate revenue, and invest in research and development to drive innovation. By fulfilling these responsibilities, stakeholders contribute to the overall socioeconomic growth of societies.

Government entities fulfill a different set of responsibilities, centered around regulation, public welfare, and governance. Governments are responsible for creating and enforcing laws and regulations that promote fair competition, protect individuals' rights, and ensure environmental sustainability. They are also accountable for providing essential public services like healthcare, education, and infrastructure.

In terms of the economic sphere, governments bear the responsibility to create a conducive environment for businesses to thrive. This involves implementing policies that encourage entrepreneurship, attracting investments, and fostering innovation. Governments also play a crucial role in levelling the playing field by preventing monopolistic practices and promoting competition.

Individuals, as the final group of stakeholders, have their own set of responsibilities to fulfill. While they may not possess the same level of influence or resources as businesses or governments, individuals still have the agency to make choices that impact society. At the most fundamental level, individuals have a responsibility to abide by the laws and regulations set forth by the government. This includes paying taxes, respecting the rights of others, and acting in accordance with the social norms and values of their communities.

Individuals also have a broader set of responsibilities that extend beyond legal obligations. This includes participating in democratic processes, such as voting in elections or engaging in grassroots activism. By doing so, individuals can influence government policies and hold elected officials accountable, shaping the trajectory of societies.

Furthermore, individuals bear the responsibility of being engaged and active members of their communities. They can contribute to positive social change by volunteering, supporting local businesses, and acting in environmentally responsible ways. Ultimately, it is through the collective actions of individuals that societies can progress and address pressing challenges.

In conclusion, the responsibilities of stakeholders, governments, and individuals are interconnected and interdependent. Stakeholders have an ethical and practical responsibility towards the broader community, while governments have a duty to regulate, govern, and provide essential services. Individuals, though possessing less power and resources, play a crucial role in shaping societies through their decisions and actions. By recognizing and fulfilling their respective responsibilities, these entities contribute to societies that are inclusive, sustainable, and prosperous.

- Discussion on intergenerational justice and the moral imperative to protect the environment

Intergenerational justice refers to the ethical principle that present generations have a moral obligation to ensure the fair distribution of resources and a sustainable environment for future generations. It involves considering the impact of our actions on the well-being and rights of future generations. This concept assumes that we have duties towards those who are not yet born.

One crucial aspect of intergenerational justice is the preservation and protection of our environment. The health and vitality of our planet directly affect future generations' lives and their ability to access resources. Therefore, we have a moral imperative to act now to protect the environment to ensure the rights and well-being of future individuals.

There are several reasons why the preservation of the environment is crucial from an intergenerational justice perspective. Firstly, present generations have a duty to ensure the availability of essential resources like clean air and water, fertile soil, and a stable climate. These resources are necessary for the survival and well-being of human beings, as well as other animal and plant species. By protecting these resources, we guarantee that future generations have access to them and can lead a dignified life.

Secondly, our actions with regard to the environment can have long-lasting and irreversible effects. For instance, the emissions of greenhouse gases lead to climate change, altering weather patterns and causing extreme events like hurricanes, droughts, and floods. These changes bring about negative consequences for human societies, including food and water scarcity, displacement, and increased health risks. By actively working to reduce our impact on the environment, we mitigate the severity of such consequences for the generations to come.

Thirdly, intergenerational justice urges us to uphold the principles of fairness and equity. Many environmental issues, such as pollution and resource depletion, disproportionately affect marginalized communities, both in the present and future. By neglecting to address these issues, we perpetuate social, economic, and environmental injustices. By striving for environmental sustainability, we aim to ensure equal opportunities and a just distribution of resources and benefits within and between generations.

Moreover, moral theories, such as contractualism, consequentialism, and deontology, uphold the importance of protecting the environment from an intergenerational justice perspective. Contractualism argues that we should act in ways that future generations would reasonably accept if they had a say in decision-making today. Thus, if we fail to protect the environment, future generations would deem our actions as immoral. Consequentialism asserts that we should act in ways that promote the greatest amount of overall well-being. By preserving the environment, we ensure the well-being of future individuals who will inherit a healthier planet. Lastly, deontology emphasizes the importance of moral duties and principles. It argues that protecting the environment is a fundamental moral obligation because it respects the rights of future individuals to a livable environment.

In conclusion, intergenerational justice demands that we take responsibility and protect the environment for the sake of future generations. This extends beyond our short-term interests and requires us to adopt sustainable practices and policies. By preserving the environment, we ensure the availability of essential resources, mitigate irreversible damage, uphold fairness and equity, and conform to moral principles. It is our moral duty to protect the environment and fulfill our obligation towards future generations.

- Examination of ethical frameworks guiding climate change actions and decision-making processes

Climate change is one of the most pressing global challenges of our time. Its impacts are already being felt in various parts of the world, as evidenced by extreme weather events, rising sea levels, and more frequent and intense heatwaves. In order to address this urgent issue, it is essential to have a clear understanding of the ethical frameworks that guide climate change actions and decision-making processes.

One of the main ethical frameworks that guide climate change actions is the consequentialist approach. Consequentialism is a moral theory that focuses on the outcomes or consequences of actions. From a consequentialist perspective, the ethicality of climate change actions is assessed based on their overall impact on human well-being and the natural environment. This framework is often associated with utilitarianism, which argues that actions should be evaluated based on their ability to maximize the overall happiness or well-being of individuals.

In the context of climate change, the consequentialist approach would urge policy-makers and decision-makers to take actions that minimize the negative consequences of climate change and maximize the overall well-being of future generations. This could include implementing policies that reduce greenhouse gas emissions, promoting the use of renewable energy sources, and enhancing resilience to climate change impacts. Proponents of this framework argue that inaction or insufficient action on climate change would result in severe negative consequences, such as widespread human suffering, loss of biodiversity, and irreversible damage to ecosystems.

Another important ethical framework for climate change actions is the deontological approach. Deontological ethics is centered around the idea that certain actions are inherently right or wrong, regardless of the consequences they may produce. From a deontological perspective, the ethicality of climate change actions is evaluated based on whether they adhere to certain moral duties or principles. In the context of climate change, principles such as fairness, justice, and respect for human rights are often invoked.

Using the deontological framework, climate change actions are considered ethical when they uphold the principles of fairness and justice, and when they respect the rights and dignity of all individuals, especially marginalized and vulnerable populations. This could involve efforts to address climate change in a way that does not disproportionately burden the poor or future generations, or promoting participatory decision-making processes that respect the rights of indigenous peoples and local communities.

Finally, the virtue ethics framework is also relevant to climate change actions and decision-making processes. Virtue ethics focuses on the character traits and virtues that individuals and institutions should cultivate to promote ethical behavior. In the context of climate change, virtues such as responsibility, prudence, and solidarity are often emphasized.

From a virtue ethics perspective, climate change actions are considered ethical when they reflect virtuous character traits and promote the well-being of both present and future generations. This could involve cultivating a sense of responsibility and accountability among policymakers and decision-makers, adopting long-term thinking and planning, and promoting solidarity and cooperation at local, national, and international levels.

In conclusion, the examination of ethical frameworks guiding climate change actions and decision-making processes reveals the complexity and multidimensionality of this global challenge. Consequentialist, deontological, and virtue ethics frameworks all provide valuable insights and considerations in the quest for ethically sound climate change policies. Integrating these ethical frameworks into decision-making processes can help ensure that climate change actions are guided by moral principles and promote the well-being and justice for both present and future generations.

Chapter 16: Conclusion

- Reflection on the urgent need for action to address Arctic warming

Arctic warming is an urgent and critical issue that demands immediate attention and concrete action. The relentless increase in temperatures in this fragile polar region is causing widespread environmental, ecological, and socio-economic consequences, not just within the Arctic but also on a global scale. It is high time that we reflect upon the urgency of this situation and consider the dire consequences of inaction.

First and foremost, the Arctic acts as a natural cooling system for the Earth due to its extensive ice cover, which reflects a significant amount of solar radiation back into space. However, this delicate balance is being disrupted by the rapid melting of ice and snow in the region. The consequences of this accelerated melting are profound. As the bright surface of the ice is lost, the darker ocean surface becomes exposed, absorbing more heat and exacerbating the warming effect. This creates a dangerous feedback loop, reinforcing further ice melt and compounding the rate of warming. If left unchecked, this feedback loop could trigger irreversible changes in global climate patterns.

The impacts of Arctic warming ripple beyond its immediate vicinity. The loss of reflective ice surfaces accelerates the overall global warming, thus contributing to the rising sea levels and increasingly erratic weather patterns witnessed worldwide. Coastal communities are already experiencing the devastating consequences of sea-level rise, with heightened vulnerability to flooding and storm surges. Additionally, extreme weather events, such as hurricanes and cyclones, hold the potential to become more frequent and intense due to the disruption of normal weather patterns caused by the Arctic warming.

Furthermore, Arctic warming poses grave risks to the delicate ecosystems thriving in the polar region. Species such as polar bears, walruses, and seals heavily rely on the sea ice for their survival, using it as a platform for hunting, breeding, and resting. With the retreat of the ice, these species are facing unprecedented challenges in finding adequate habitat and food sources. Consequently, their population numbers are dwindling, resulting in irreversible biodiversity loss.

The socio-economic repercussions of Arctic warming cannot be undermined either. Indigenous communities inhabiting the Arctic region, dependant on traditional practices like hunting and fishing, are starting to face severe disruptions and threats to their way of life. The melting of permafrost is destabilizing infrastructure, such as roads, airports, and buildings, making daily life increasingly challenging. Moreover, the opening of previously ice-covered waterways due to reduced ice extent opens up the Arctic to extractive industries, fueling further anthropogenic greenhouse gas emissions and exacerbating climate change.

In light of these alarming implications, urgent action is the need of the hour. Global cooperation is necessary to reduce greenhouse gas emissions, decrease reliance on fossil fuels, and transition towards renewable energy sources. Policies focused on stricter regulations and international agreements to limit emissions are essential to mitigate the impacts of Arctic warming.

Furthermore, it is crucial to invest in long-term monitoring and research efforts to better understand the complex interactions between the Arctic and global climate systems. Adequate funding and support for scientific studies will provide crucial data to drive informed policy decisions and the development of effective adaptation measures.

Finally, engaging and empowering local communities, particularly indigenous peoples, in decision-making processes and initiatives is integral. Indigenous knowledge and traditional practices hold valuable insights into coexisting sustainably with nature and adapting to changing conditions. Their involvement ensures that policies and actions are inclusive, equitable, and sustainable, benefiting both local communities and the environment.

In conclusion, the urgency of addressing Arctic warming cannot be overstated. The consequences of inaction are severe, affecting not only the Arctic region but also the entire planet. We must reflect upon the gravity of this situation and commit wholeheartedly to taking the necessary actions. The time for rhetoric is over; the time for meaningful and decisive action is now.

- Call to action for individuals, communities, and governments to step up their efforts

Addressing the urgency of the current global challenges such as climate change, social inequality, economic instability, and political conflicts, it has become increasingly important for individuals, communities, and governments to step up their efforts. The need to take action has never been more evident, and it is essential that we harness our collective power to address these issues head-on.

To begin with, individuals play a crucial role in driving positive change. Each and every one of us has the power to make a difference, no matter how small or insignificant it may seem. By making sustainable choices in our daily lives, such as consuming responsibly, reducing waste, and embracing renewable energy sources, we can contribute significally to mitigating climate change. Moreover, engaging in active citizenship and participating in civic movements can amplify our impact on issues ranging from social equity to political reform, ultimately fostering a healthier and more just society.

However, it is not enough for individuals to act in isolation. Communities must come together, united by a shared purpose and commitment to a better future. By organizing grassroots movements, community projects, and initiatives, we can create a network of support that empowers individuals and amplifies their voices. By strengthening community resilience, promoting inclusivity, and directing resources toward sustainable development, communities can shape a sustainable and thriving future for their members.

Yet, the responsibility to create meaningful change should not be solely shouldered by individuals and communities. Governments, as institutions with the power to enforce policies and regulations, have the obligation to prioritize the greater good and overcome short-term interests for the benefit of everyone. Policies that encourage sustainable practices, fund renewable energy research, support social programs, and promote peace can dramatically accelerate progress towards a more sustainable and equitable society. Governments should focus on fostering international cooperation, building strong global partnerships, and setting ambitious targets to address the pressing global challenges we face.

Moreover, to effectively tackle these challenges, collaboration between individuals, communities, and governments is paramount. By engaging in open dialogue, finding common ground, and pooling resources, remarkable progress can be achieved. Public-private partnerships can play a particularly significant role in leveraging the knowledge, expertise, and resources of both sectors to drive innovation and implement sustainable solutions.

In conclusion, the call to action for individuals, communities, and governments to step up their efforts in addressing global challenges is imperative. Taking action on an individual level, fostering community empowerment, and demanding accountable and responsible governance can catalyze considerable change. It is time we act together, recognizing the urgency of the situation, and shining a light on our shared future. Let us stand hand in hand to safeguard our planet, ensure social justice, and build a better world for generations to come.

- Exploration of potential climate-positive pathways for the future of the Arctic

The future of the Arctic is of utmost importance for global climate stability. Due to its unique geographical location, the Arctic is experiencing the most immediate and pronounced impacts of climate change. The rapidly melting sea ice, rising temperatures, and thawing permafrost in the region are not only affecting ecosystems and indigenous communities but also having implications for the rest of the planet.

However, amidst the gloomy predictions and challenges lies a silver lining-the potential for climate-positive pathways that can be pursued to ensure the future well-being of the Arctic and the world. These pathways are focused on minimizing further damage to the region and actively working towards reversing the effects of climate change.

One such pathway involves a significant reduction in greenhouse gas emissions to mitigate the warming of the Arctic. This can be achieved by transitioning away from fossil fuels and investing heavily in renewable energy sources such as solar, wind, and hydroelectric power. Implementing strict regulations and carbon pricing mechanisms can incentivize industries and individuals to decrease their carbon footprint. Additionally, intergovernmental collaboration is crucial to ensure that emission reduction targets are met on a global scale.

Furthermore, targeted efforts to restore damaged ecosystems and reforest areas in the Arctic can play a significant role in the climate-positive pathway. Afforestation and reforestation have proven to be effective methods for carbon sequestration, with trees absorbing and storing carbon dioxide from the atmosphere. Such initiatives can also provide habitat restoration for indigenous flora and fauna, thus promoting biodiversity.

The melting of the Arctic sea ice presents an opportunity for exploring sustainable and low-carbon transportation routes, known as the Arctic shipping lane. This lane would significantly reduce travel distances and carbon emissions for vessels traveling between Europe and Asia compared to traditional shipping routes. However, caution must be exercised to minimize the risks of environmental damage from increased shipping activity in the region.

In addition to these measures, the preservation of Arctic cultures and their traditional knowledge is vital for a climate-positive future. Indigenous communities have a deep understanding of the Arctic environment and possess valuable insights into how to live sustainably in harmony with nature. Their traditional knowledge, combined with modern scientific advancements, can drive innovative solutions to address the challenges posed by climate change.

Investments in research and development are also crucial to paving the way for a climate-positive Arctic. By supporting scientific endeavors to better understand Arctic ecosystems, dynamics, and climate processes, we can make informed decisions and implement appropriate policies. This includes studying the impacts of climate change on Arctic wildlife, the effects of thawing permafrost on greenhouse gas emissions, and developing adaptation strategies for indigenous communities.

Lastly, international cooperation and strong governance mechanisms are essential for the successful implementation of climate-positive pathways in the Arctic. The Arctic Council, an intergovernmental forum composed of Arctic nations, has been instrumental in facilitating dialogue, coordinating actions, and fostering collaboration in the region. Strengthening and expanding the role of the Arctic Council could bolster climate-positive efforts and ensure the sustainable future of the region.

Overall, the exploration of potential climate-positive pathways for the future of the Arctic holds immense promise. By reducing greenhouse gas emissions, restoring ecosystems, promoting sustainable transportation, preserving indigenous cultures, investing in research, and enhancing international cooperation, we can work towards a future where the Arctic thrives, and global climate stability is secured. The time to act is now, and the Arctic offers both the urgency and the opportunity to make a positive and lasting impact.

- Recapitulation of the importance of understanding global warming in the Arctic

Understanding global warming in the Arctic is of paramount importance due to its direct implications not only on the region itself but also on the rest of the planet. The Arctic, consisting of sea ice, permafrost, and unique ecosystems, serves as a barometer for measuring the impacts of global climate change. Hence, a thorough comprehension of the dynamics of warming in this region becomes an essential tool in tackling the global environmental crisis.

One of the significant consequences of global warming in the Arctic is the rapid decline of sea ice. The Arctic sea ice cover has been shrinking considerably over the past few decades, with record lows in the extent and thickness of ice. This reduction in sea ice has numerous cascading effects. Firstly, it contributes to the rise in global sea levels as the melting ice adds vast amounts of freshwater to the oceans. This threatens coastal communities worldwide, increasing the risks of flooding and undermining coastal infrastructure. Moreover, the diminishing sea ice hampers the ability of polar bears and other iconic Arctic species to find food and navigate across their habitat, endangering their existence. This loss of biodiversity has severe consequences for both ecosystem stability and human societies that rely on these resources for sustenance.

Another critical consequence of warming in the Arctic is the thawing of permafrost. Permafrost is a layer of permanently frozen ground that stores massive amounts of carbon in the form of decaying organic matter. With rising temperatures, permafrost degradation accelerates, releasing greenhouse gases into the atmosphere. In particular, the release of methane, a potent greenhouse gas, from thawing permafrost can trigger a positive feedback loop, exacerbating global warming. Furthermore, the erosion of permafrost undermines the stability of infrastructure such as buildings, roads, and pipelines, affecting communities and industries operating in the Arctic.

Understanding global warming in the Arctic is vital not only for assessing the current impacts but also for predicting future scenarios. The changes occurring in the Arctic serve as warning signs for the direction and magnitude of climate change globally. The melting of Arctic ice reflects a warming trend that is linked to the increase in greenhouse gas emissions from human activities. Therefore, investigating Arctic climate patterns, ice dynamics, and ecosystem shifts contributes crucially to our knowledge of the complex climate system as a whole.

Furthermore, the Arctic plays a significant role in regulating global climate through its influence on oceanic and atmospheric circulation patterns. Changes in sea ice cover and ocean temperatures disrupt these circulations, thereby impacting weather patterns at lower latitudes. The Arctic acts as a global air conditioner, helping to cool the planet by reflecting sunlight back into space. However, as sea ice declines, the absorption of sunlight by dark ocean surfaces increases, leading to further warming. This interconnectedness between the Arctic and the broader planet demands an understanding of the dynamics at play to make informed decisions on mitigating global warming.

Ultimately, an in-depth comprehension of global warming in the Arctic is crucial for our ability to face the challenges of climate change adequately. It provides vital information for policymakers, scientists, and societies at large to develop effective strategies for reducing greenhouse gas emissions, adapting to changing environmental conditions, and preserving the unique Arctic ecosystems. Furthermore, the global consequences of Arctic warming act as a call to action, urging the international community to take collective responsibility in safeguarding the planet and combating the climate crisis.

- Final thoughts on the potential consequences of inaction

And so, as we come to the end of this discussion on the potential consequences of inaction, it becomes apparent that our unperturbed apathy holds grave repercussions both for ourselves and for future generations. The inertia that surrounds us, that grips us in its suffocating embrace, can lull us into a false sense of security, yet it blinds us to the imminent dangers that loom on the horizon.

Inaction in the face of pressing global challenges such as climate change, inequality, and political unrest, would undoubtedly precipitate a downward spiral that only promises disaster. Our Earth, already burdened by the excessive demands of human activity, is gasping for breath as we stand idly by, allowing the scorched earth to crack beneath our collective inaction.

Perhaps the most immediate and evident consequence of our inaction lies within the realm of environmental degradation. Global temperatures continue to rise, ice caps are melting, and extreme weather events become increasingly common. The dire warnings of scientists are drowned out by the cacophony of denial and skepticism from those who refuse to acknowledge the urgency of the situation. Failure to act will result in irreversible damage, rendering vast areas of this beautiful blue planet uninhabitable, and eliminating numerous species that we share our home with.

But it is not only the environment that bears the brunt of our inaction; social and economic divisions are also exacerbated by our refusal to act. The gap between the haves and have-nots widens, creating a deeply divided society where opportunities for success become a luxury restricted to the few. This stifles innovation, creativity, and progress, leaving countless talents and aspirations unfulfilled, and ultimately leading us down a path towards instability and conflict.

Inaction, or the lack of proactive measures, not only perpetuates existing systemic injustice but also enables the erosion of democracy and freedom.

Political inaction in the face of rising authoritarianism and threats to universal human rights leaves marginalized communities exposed to discrimination, persecution, and oppression. The silence of the powerful, the turning of a blind eye, entrenches the oppressive systems that thrive on unchecked power, further perpetuating the cycles of injustice.

Ultimately, the consequences of inaction will seep into every aspect of our lives. The legacy we leave behind for future generations will be marred by regret, as our failure to act anchors them in a world mired by the consequences of our indifference. Our children, grandchildren, and generations yet to come will bear the consequences of our inaction, of the choices we make today.

In light of these potential consequences, we must be spurred into action. We must overcome our complacency and recognize that the future lies in our hands. It is up to each and every one of us to demand change, to hold our leaders accountable, and to challenge the status quo. Through collective action, we can rewrite the narrative, breaking free from the chains of inaction that shackle us.

The stakes are high, and time is of the essence. We no longer have the luxury of standing idly by, for inaction is not a choice but a dereliction of our duties as stewards of this planet and custodians of humanity. Let us not be defined by our inaction, but rather by our resolve to create a better future for ourselves and those who will inherit this world.

- Encouragement for continued research, advocacy, and collaboration for a sustainable future

In today's rapidly changing world, the need for sustainable development has become more urgent than ever before. With the challenges posed by climate change, dwindling natural resources, and social inequality becoming increasingly evident, it is imperative that we take action to ensure a sustainable future for ourselves and future generations.

Research plays a vital role in tackling these complex issues. By studying the environment, developing innovative technologies, and analyzing societal trends, researchers can provide valuable insights into how we can create a more sustainable world. Their work helps us understand the root causes of environmental degradation and social injustice, guiding us towards effective solutions.

However, research alone is not enough. Advocacy is crucial for raising awareness and generating support for sustainable development initiatives. Advocates can help translate research findings into actionable policies and influence public opinion on pressing sustainability issues. Whether it be media campaigns, grassroots organizing, or lobbying efforts, advocacy adds an important dimension to the conversation, pushing for systemic change that can promote positive environmental and social outcomes.

Furthermore, collaboration is an essential ingredient in achieving sustainability goals. No single entity can address the complex challenges we face in isolation. It requires cooperation between governments, businesses, non-profit organizations, and communities to devise comprehensive and effective strategies. Collaboration fosters the sharing of knowledge, resources, and best practices, making it possible to tackle problems more efficiently. By working together, we can leverage the strengths of different stakeholders and create synergistic solutions that have a far-reaching impact.

To encourage continued research, advocacy, and collaboration for a sustainable future, it is important to recognize and appreciate the progress that has already been made. There have been countless success stories, where research has led to breakthrough technologies, advocacy has inspired policy changes, and collaboration has brought about transformative partnerships. By highlighting these achievements, we can motivate individuals and organizations to stay committed and motivated to contribute to sustainable development.

In addition, it is crucial to provide support and funding for those engaged in sustainability-related work. Researchers, advocates, and collaboratives often face significant challenges, including limited resources, public skepticism, and bureaucratic hurdles. By investing in their efforts, we can create an overall enabling environment that empowers individuals and organizations to drive positive change.

The road towards a sustainable future may be long and challenging, but the rewards are immeasurable. The benefits of sustainable development stretch beyond environmental conservation, encompassing social justice, economic stability, and improved quality of life for all. By continuing research, advocacy, and collaboration, we are investing in a brighter and more equitable future.

In conclusion, the importance of continued research, advocacy, and collaboration for a sustainable future cannot be overstated. They form the backbone of efforts to address climate change, protect natural resources, and build a more equitable society. By encouraging and supporting individuals and organizations involved in these endeavors, we foster a collective commitment to sustainability that can truly make a difference. Let us persevere and remain resolute in our pursuit of a better, more sustainable world.

* 9 7 9 8 2 2 4 9 6 9 9 1 3 *